THOUGHTS ON LANDSCAPE PAINTING

4rd Edition

Compiled by
Niles Nordquist

All rights reserved. No part of this book may be
reproduced, stored in a retrieval system,
transmitted in any form or by any means,
electronic, mechanical, photocopying, recording or
otherwise, without the prior written permission of
Niles Nordquist, except for the quotations

Nordquist, Niles
Thoughts on Landscape Painting, 4th Edition

ISBN-13:978-1979956055
ISBN-10:1979956057

Art Reference

The HeArt Endeavor Press
www.heartendevor.org.
2017

Cover art: "The Continental Divide", Niles Nordquist

TABLE OF CONTENTS

INTRODUCTION

Bibliography

GENERAL PAINTING 1
Purpose of Art and Painting 1
The Artist 3
Art Patrons 4
Learning to Paint 5
On Rules and Advice 7
Mistakes 9
Copying Others 11

THE PROCESS OF PAINTING 14
Strategy 14
Tricks 14
Viewing the scene and canvas 14
Squinting 14
Standing and Viewing 15
Seeing 15
Conservation and Reserve 17
Blocking In 19
Modeling Shapes and Details 21
Speed 21
Studio Painting 23
First Things 24
Finishing 26

Thoughts on Landscape Painting

Technical Aids 29
Photography 29
Camera Obscura and Grids 32
Mirrors 34
Miscellaneous 34

Landscape Painting From Nature 35
Philosophy 35
Landscape Subjects 38
Observation 40
Studies and Pochades 42
Dealing With the Sun 44
Vantage Point 45
Painting Outside 46

Brushwork 48
Brushes 48
Brushstrokes 49
Palette Knife 56

Materials 58
Oil Paint 58
Materials and Tools 59

COMPOSITION 60
Subject 60
Subject in Context **60**
Choosing a Subject **60**
Interpreting the Subject 63
Augmenting the Subject 64

Thoughts on Landscape Painting

Arrangement 65
Approach 65
Shapes and Masses 69
Focal Point and Center of Interest 73
Repetition 77
Gradation 78
Line 78
Simplification 80
Balance 81
Unity and Variety 82
Golden Section 84
Drawing 85
Texture 86
Perspective 87

Visual Movement 88
Visual Movement Theory 88
Lines of Motion 88
Diagonal Movement 92
Visual Traps 93

Light And Shadow 96
Light / Shadow Theory 96
Light / Shadow Contrast 97
Placing Light and Shadows 97
Observing Light and Shadow 98
Shadow Color 99

Thoughts on Landscape Painting

Values 100
Value Theory 100
Value Contrasts 103
Value Placement 105
Value Gradation 107

Color 108
Color Theory 108
Color of Light 110
Selecting Colors 112
Placing Color 114
Mixing Color 117
Color Harmony 119

Edges 121
Edge Theory 121
Creating Edges 124

Thoughts on Landscape Painting

QUOTATION BIBLIOGRAPHY

Albert, Greg, *The Simple Secret To Better Painting,* North Light Books, 2003

American Artist Magazine, Wooters, Chad

Audette, Anna, *The Blank Canvas,* Shambhala Press, 1993 (Josef Albers, Leo Steinberg, Robert Motherwell)

Bayles, David, *Art & Fear,* Capra Press, 1993 (Adam Gopnik, Ben Shahn)

Bell, Adrienne Baxter, *George Inness and The Visionary Landscape,* George Braziller, Publishers, New York, 2003

Boorstin, Daniel J., *The Creators,* Random House, New York, 1992.

Brown, Clint, *Artist to Artist,* Jackson Creek Press, 1998

Brown, Harley, *Eternal Truths For Every Artist,* International Artist Publishers, 2002

Budicin, John, *Workshop*, Taos, New Mexico, 2001

Buechner, Thomas, *How I Paint - Secrets of a Sunday Painter*, Harry N. Abrams Publisher, 2000

Carlson, John, *Carlson's Guide to Landscape Painting*, Dover Publications, 1929

Cateura, Linda, *Painting Secrets from a Master - David Leffel*, Watson-Guptill Publications, 1995

Cox, Kenyon, *What is painting?* (1856-1919), Norton Publications, 1988

Christensen, Scott, Workshop Oregon, 2001

Churchill, Winston, *Painting as a Pastime*, Levenger Press, 1932

Craig, Diana, A Miscellany of Artists' Wisdom, Running Press, 1993 (Cennino Cennini (1435) Il Libro Dell'arte, Giorgio De Chirico, (1888-1978), Marcus, Cicero, (106-43 B.C.), Plato (c. 427-347 B.C.), Giorgio Vasari (1568) Lives Of The Artists, William Williams, (17th C) On The Mechanic Of Oil Colors, John Elsum, (1704) The Art Of Painting After The Italian Manner, Joseph Farington, (1747-1821) The Diaries Of Joseph Farington)

Curtis, David, *A Light Touch, Successful Paintings in Oils*, David & Charles Publishers, 1994

De Leeuw, Ronald, *The Letters Of Vincent Van Gogh (1853-1890)*, Penguin Books, 1996

Dow, Arthur W., *Composition*, University Of California Press, 1923

Dunstan, Bernard, *Composing Your Paintings*, Watson-Guptill Publications, 1971

Gauguin, Paul, The *Intimate Journals Of Paul Gauguin (1848-1903)*, KPI, Ltd., 1923

Gauss, Charles E., *The Aesthetic Theories of French Artists*, Johns Hopkins Press, 1966, Manet 1863, Gustav Corbet 1855, Renoir 1884, Cezanne 1878, Matisse 1908

Glenbow Museum, *Carl Rungius: Artist & Sportsman*, Warwick Publishing, Toronto, 2001

Goerschner, Ted, Oil *Painting: The Workshop Experience*, North Light Books, 1996

Gruppe, Emile, *Gruppe On Painting - Direct Techniques In Oil*, Watson-Guptill Publications, 1976

Hamerton, Philip G., *Thoughts About Art*, Robert Brothers, 1882

Handell, Albert and Leslie, *Intuitive Composition*, Watson-Guptill Publications, 1989

Harvey, Eleanor, *The Painted Sketch*, Harry N. Abrams Publisher, 1998 (Fredrick Church, Thomas Cole)

Henri, Robert, *The Art Spirit* (1865-1929), Harper & Row, 1923

Hongnian, Zhang, *The Yin/Yang of Painting*, Watson-Guptill Publications, 2000

International Artist Magazine, Clyde Aspevig, John Budicin, Josh Elliott, Daniel Goozee, Albert Handell, Ken Knight, Bonnie Paruch, Camille Przewodek, Stephen Quiller, Bob Rohm, Matt Smith, Ken Strong)

Kendall, Richard, editor, *Degas By Himself (1834-1917)*, Chartwell Books, Inc., 1987

Kendall, Richard, editor, *Monet by Himself*, editor, Barnes & Noble Books, New York, 2004

King, Jennifer, Expressing *The Visual Language Of The Landscape*, International Artist Publishers, 2002 (Dean Mitchell, Matt Smith)

Komar, Vitaly, *Painting By Numbers*, University Of California Press, 1997

MacCurdy, Edward, *The Notebooks Of Leonardo Da Vinci (1452-1519)*, Konecky & Konecky, 1906

Macpherson, Kevin, *Fill Your Paintings with Light and Color*, North Light Books, 1996

McCaw, Dan, *A Proven Strategy for Creating Great Art*, International Artist Publishers, 2003

Meyer, Laure, *Masters Of The English Landscape*, Terrail, 1993 (Alexander Cozens, (1750), Thomas Gainsborough, (1750)

Merriam-Webster Guide to Quotations, Langenscheidt, New York, 1995

OPA, Oil Painters of America, On-line Blog, Various Authors, through 2017

The Oxford Dictionary of Quotations, 2nd Ed, Oxford University Press, New York, 1966

Payne, Edgar, *Composition Outdoor Painting (1882- 1947)*, Payne Studios, 1941

Peel, Edgar, *The Painter Joaquin Sorolla Y Bastida (1863-1923)*, San Diego Museum of Art, 1989

Poore, Henry, *Composition In Art*, Dover Publications, 1967

Protter, Eric, *Painters on Painting*, Dover Publications, Mineola, New York, 1997, William Blake (1757-1825), Jean Baptiste Camille Corot (1796-1875), Camille Pissarro (1831-1903), Winslow Homer (1836-1910)

Reid, Charles, *Painting what you want to see*, Watson-Guptill Publications, 1987

Reid, Charles, *Worshop*, San Diego, California, 1995

Reynolds, Robert, *Painting Nature's Peaceful Places*, North Light Books, 1993

Ruskin, John, *Modern Painters - Book I*, The Blackfriars Publishing Co., 1857

Ruskin, John, *Modern Painters - Book V*, The Blackfriars Publishing Co., 1857

Ruskin, John, *The Elements of Drawing*, The Blackfriars Publishing Co., 1857

Ruskin, John, *The Two Paths*, The Blackfriars Publishing Co., 1857

Schmid, Richard, *Alla Prima - Everything I Know About Painting*, Stove Prairie Press, 1999

Schneider, Norbert, *Vermeer, Vieled Emotions (1632-1675)*, Barnes &.Noble, 2001

Smuskiewicz, Ted, *Oil Painting - Step By Step*, North Light Books, 1992

Spencer, John, *Leon Battista Alberti On Painting (1436)*, Yale University Press, 1956

Strisik, Paul, *Capturing Light In Oils*, North Light Books, 1995

Sloan, John, *John Sloan on Drawing and Painting (Gist of Art)*, (1871-1951), Dover Publications, 1944

The Artist's Magazine, (Gary Akers, David Arsenault, Ed Brickler, Doug Dawson, Tim Iverson, Jane Jones, Butch Krieger, Kevin Macpherson, Frank Nieset, Valerie Shesko, Bill Tilton)

Thoughts on Landscape Painting

Webb, Frank, *Strengthen Your Paintings With Dynamic Composition*, North Light Books, 1994

Wellington, Hubert, *The Journal Of Eugene Delacroix (1798-1863)*, Phaidon Press, 1951

Whisson, Colley, *Creating Impressionist Landscapes in Oil*, International Artist Publishers, 2001

Wilson-Bareau, Juliet, editor, *Manet by Himself*, Barnes & Noble Books, New York, 2004

Introduction

This work is a compilation of thoughts on landscape painting from artists and philosophers or both. It extends over a period of twenty-five hundred years including quotations primarily from European and American artists.

The references come from more than eighty books, articles, and workshops. This required the review of more than twenty-five-thousand pages of text. Some citations extend back to classical Greece. Others are found in currently published art instruction books and magazine articles. All of these sources are valuable. I have only extracted a few statements from the treasures held in each of these resources. Each is worthy of acquisition by the reader.

The primary focus of the selected quotations is the **oil painting of landscapes**. Some references to other mediums and subjects are included as needed to complete the intent of the statements. Both plein air and studio work is considered.

Each citation is identified as to its source. In addition, if the work is from a deceased author, dates are provided. I have chosen to include only text and not graphic elements. This is deliberate on my part, as my intention is to allow the reader to visualize the statements made. Often, statements are at odds with each other, giving a contrasting opinion. In other cases, concepts that appear to be new to the last hundred years may be seen as hundreds if not thousands of years old.

This work is organized into three primary sections: General Painting, The Process of Painting, and Composition. Many topical subdivisions are included in each section. The sequence of the quotations within each section is not necessarily organized into a continuum.

The bibliography is included at the beginning of this work. It offers the reader a general idea of the range of consideration that is included. Many of these books remain in print. Others are out of print or are rare books.

I have enjoyed this adventure and offer a passage that summarizes the spirit of my endeavor:

> To those who are looking for
> suggestions which might aid them
> developing their own ideas, skill
> or appreciation, this little volume
> is fraternally presented.
>   Payne, Edgar (1882- 1947)

Thoughts on Landscape Painting

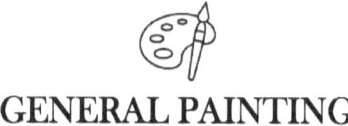

GENERAL PAINTING

Purpose of Art and Painting

By the art of painting we make another house, a sort of man-made dream produced for those who are awake   Plato (c. 427-347 B.C.) Craig

Painting is concerned with all the ten attributes of sight, namely darkness, brightness, substance and colour, form and place, remoteness and nearness, movement and rest; and it is with these attributes that my small book will be interwoven.   Da Vinci (1452-1519) MacCurdy

Leo Steinberg - All art is infested by other art. Audette

I always say interpretation, never imitation. My reason for doing so is, first, that good art rarely imitates; it usually only describes or explains. But my second and chief reason is that good art always consists of two things: First, the observation of fact; secondly, the manifesting of human design and authority in the way that fact is told. Great and good art must unite the two.   John Ruskin - Paths 1857

The aim of painting: to give pleasure, good will and fame to the painter more than riches. If painters will follow this, their painting will hold the eyes and the soul of the observer. Alberti 1436 Spencer
Preconceived ideas are death to a creative mind. That is why you must study nature often. Learn to see the things that best describe the character of an object.   Christensen

Every production of genius is the production of enthusiasm. Yet enthusiasm should never lead beyond good taste or judgment.

Thoughts on Landscape Painting

Knowledge or reason always needs to check over enthusiasm. Payne 1941

In landscapes, the painter should give the suggestion of a fairer creation than we know. The details, the prose of nature he should omit, and give us only the spirit and the splendor.   Ralph Waldo Emerson

How strongly do new paintings usually appeal to us at first for the beauty and variety of their colours, and yet it is the old and rough picture that holds our attention.   Cicero (106-43 B.C.) Craig

To become truly immortal a work of art must escape all human limits: logic and common sense will only interfere. But once these barriers are broken it will enter the regions of childhood vision and dream. De Chirico (1888-1978) Craig

Art is paradoxically aristocratic and democratic. Aristocratic because artworks are the most valued objects we rescue from history's scrap heap. Democratic because no one needs a license, diploma, or a membership to practice art. No door is closed because of race, age, gender or class. Webb
Things Have Bulk—Art Has Form.   Sloan 1944
Challenge keeps painting from becoming a craft. Charles Reid - Workshop

All "realistic" painting is actually abstract. The painter uses paint configurations, squiggles, pigments, and these purport to be flesh, apples, grass, air, space and so forth. The so-called abstract painter actually is very concrete.   Drippings are actual drippings! Paint shot on the canvas or splashed is just that. Rents, holes, sawn pieces are, likewise, exactly that. Leffel

The work of most occupations goes up in smoke. A fine work of art will please for several lifetimes. Webb

Thoughts on Landscape Painting

The world offers vastly more support to work it already understands — namely, art that's already been around for a generation or a century. Bayles

What I dream of is an art of equilibrium, purity, and tranquility, without disquieting or disturbing subjects. Matisse 1908, Gauss

The Artist

We artists work in a realm where instinct and emotion and intelligence mingle bewilderingly, and what works in one case may not always work in another.   Schmid

Never let it be supposed that anyone can be a good painter if he does not clearly understand what he is attempting to do. Alberti 1436 Spencer

An artist should want nothing of commonplace, continually searching for something outside of mediocrity. Be innovative, the imaginative soul sees more that it can possibly portray. Christensen
For most artists, making good art depends upon making lots of art. Bayles

He who cannot respond to his emotions with some reasonable guidance is incapable of expressing himself in an artistic manner. Payne 1941

There is great injustice among the fine arts. The great and the famous are not the same persons. Great painters can go unnoticed while aesthetic pip-squeaks get publicity and sell well. The low taste of mass marketing and mass media trivialize art. Webb

Genius and regularity are utter enemies, and must be to the end of time. Thomas Gainsborough (1750) Meyer

Thoughts on Landscape Painting

Artists who seek for perfection in everything achieve it in nothing
Delacroix (1798-1863), Wellington

The student paints things, the mature artist paints ideas about things, or concepts. Leffel

My hand often gets tired, and my sight also; but my ambition as a painter, never.   Sorolla 1915 Peel

Art Patrons

Superficial people will be interested in superficial paintings. Webb

The viewers' concerns are not your concerns (although it's dangerously easy to adopt their attitudes.) Their job is whatever it is: to be moved by art, to be entertained by it, to make a killing off it, whatever. Your job is to learn to work on your work. Bayles

You might as well get used to this fact: Not everyone will like your work. Webb

"Post-modernist art is, above all, post-audience art." Adam Gopnik, Bayles
Perhaps a picture lives only during the time that one pulls it together as a beholder. A good creative painting calls the viewer into a collaboration. Webb

The work of the painter attempts to be pleasing to the multitude; therefore do not disdain the judgment and views of the multitude when it is possible to satisfy their opinions.   Alberti 1436 Spencer

Dear Messrs. O'Brien & Sons:

Thoughts on Landscape Painting

Gentlemen, I am in receipt of your letter inviting me to have an exhibition at your Galleries. .... At the present and for some time past I see no reason why I should paint any pictures. P.S. I will paint for money at any time. Any subject, any size.   Homer 1896, Protter

I want you to understand, sir, that I claim the right to go into any house and change a work of mine when I am not satisfied with it, and see where I can improve it. Do you think because you have paid money for a picture of mine, that it belongs to you?
Inness

The fact is that official acceptance, encouragement and rewards are seen by a certain section of the public as a guarantee of talent, and this public is accordingly predisposed for or against the accepted or rejected works. Manet, 1987, Wilson-Bareau

Learning to Paint

No one has ever quite learned how to paint. Webb

The most important ally in the study of painting is the art of thinking. Payne 1941

All art knowledge is self-taught, but it is not learned in isolation. A teacher gives you an environment and technical help. Webb

While talent is an important qualification, there is no proof of real worth in talent until it has been developed and expanded by a tremendous amount of serious study and plain hard work. Payne 1941

Each time you start a new painting, you bring to your effort everything that you have learned from every other painting you have ever done. The books you read, the formal training

Thoughts on Landscape Painting

you have had, your access to great paintings, all (should) come into play automatically.   Schmid

Start each new canvas with the idea of doing a beautiful painting and only secondly of learning to paint.   Leffel

Knowledge always precedes execution. No one can paint better than he knows how. (1) Accumulate knowledge (2) Study nature often (3) Practice continually.   Payne 1941

The greatest teacher of painting may be the pencil.   Webb

There is persistent effort to set aside most principles, inject all sorts of irrelevant ideas and adopt short cuts to lift the incompetent to fame. However, if the student expects his work to fulfill the intended purpose of art, he will have to do as someone has said, "Mix brains with paint." This means that reason or intelligence be used along with study and practice.   Payne 1941

Learn what paint will do.   Leffel

It is not for what he does, but for what he learns, that the practice is so useful. Whilst he is painting a scene under one effect, he sees it under a thousand, and is incessantly occupied in comparing them. He is always learning something which he did not intend to learn ; knowledge of all kinds being brought before him as he sits at work by the inevitable changes of the natural scene.   Hamerton 1882.

One of the problems in learning to paint is learning what your tools will do to translate what you see. Your equipment is limited to value, color, edges, and impasto. These are all the tools there are to create the illusion of reality on your canvas.   Leffel

Thoughts on Landscape Painting

Rules and Advice

The painter ought to be desirous of hearing every man's opinion as to the progress of his work.   Surely when a man is painting a picture he ought not to refuse to hear any man's opinion, for we know very well that though a man may not be a painter he may have a true conception of form.   Da Vinci 1452-1519 MacCurdy

Therefore, give to things a moderated diligence and take the advice of friends. In painting open yourself to whoever comes and hear everyone. The work of the painter attempts to be pleasing to the multitude; therefore do not disdain the judgment and views of the multitude when it is possible to satisfy their opinions.   Alberti 1436 Spencer
Ask a trusted person for a critique—try to dispassionate about this process. Don't take what they say personally because they are trying to be helpful.   Whisson

An orgy of self-expression is no more productive than blind obedience to rules.   Rudolf Arnheim   Webb

The substitution of obedience to mathematical law for sympathy with observed life is the first characteristic of the hopeless work of all ages.   John Ruskin - Paths 1857

Well composed.   Does that mean according to rule? No. Precisely the contrary. John Ruskin - Painters I 1857

We do not long remember those artists who followed the rules more diligently than anyone else. We remember those who made the art from which the "rules" inevitably follow. Bayles

Each individual must be guided by his own feeling or taste in this matter; formulas might lead to deadly repetition. But mixed up with our "feelings" about anything, there is a certain proportion of reason. Reason never produced a work of art, but in all true

Thoughts on Landscape Painting

works of art there is a certain amount of very sane reasoning (subconscious though it be).   Carlson 1929

Survey of 1001 Americans on Preferences in Paintings
AMERICA'S MOST WANTED
- Dishwasher-size (67:%)
- Paintings that are "realistic- looking" (60%).
- Outdoor scenes (88%) featuring lakes, rivers, oceans, and seas (49%)
- Persons in group (48%), fully clothed (68%), and at leisure (43%)
- Ordinary people or famous—makes no difference (50%)
- Blue (44%)
- Fall Scene (33%)
- Brush Strokes (53%)
- Colors Blended (68%)
- Soft Curves (66%) and playful, whimsical designs (49%)
- Fall Scene (33%)
- More Vibrant shades (36%)
- Wild animals in their natural setting (89%)

AMERICA'S MOST UNWANTED
- Paperback-book-size (4%)
- Paintings that are "different-looking" (30%) and feature imaginary objects (36%)
- Thick, textured surfaces (40%)
- Geometric patterns (30%)
- Sharp angles (22%) and bold, stark designs (39%)
- Darker shades (22%)
- Gold, orange, peach, teal (1%)
- Colors kept separate (18%)

                                                              Komar

They are by no means recipes for art. Dow 1923

Thoughts on Landscape Painting

Mistakes

A "mistake" done with a crisp, confident brushstroke will look better than something correct done with a flaccid brushstroke. Leffel

Painting is a series of corrections; when there are no more to be done, you're finished.   MacPherson
Learn to 'live' with the painting in the build-up stages: creativity is sometimes a long business involving constant adjustments and reappraisal. Curtis

When correcting the color of any mass, try to do it by laying into it the correcting tones in small touches, and without lifting the under paint up too much.   Carlson 1929

Doctors bury their mistakes, architects plant ivy around their mistakes, and we frame ours and send them off to juried shows. Webb

The painter who is afraid of mistakes is not going to have much fun. Webb

There is no art which has not had its beginnings in things full of errors. Nothing is at the same time both new and perfect. Alberti (paraphrasing Cicero) 1436   Audette

You can always correct an oil painting. You can't ruin it. Leffel

Don't be despondent about what you feel to be lack of progress. Good painting is not a happy accident or a matter of luck - it is the product of experience and many apparent failures. Curtis

An 'unsuccessful' painting can be the basis of a new painting. Simply scrape off any 'knobs' of color, turn the old painting upside down on the easel, make one or two construction lines or marks to represent the new subject and carry on - the result may surprise you. Curtis

Thoughts on Landscape Painting

Selections from a check list of common mistakes and difficulties: Schmid

Careless drawing (not measuring).
Too many sharp edges.
Trying to paint things instead of color shapes.
Painting more values than are necessary.
Incorrect temperature changes.
Inventing impossible color.
Miserly paint (too little).
Unsuitable brushes.
Poorly stretched canvas.
Painting over life-size without a good reason.
Allowing too little time.
Working too close, not stepping back to view your work.
Overworking what should be left alone.
Working from inadequate photos.
Poor working light.
Not squinting for values and edges.
Too many highlights.
Painting shadows too light.
Muddy (wrong temperature) color.
"Pushing" bright colors arbitrarily.
Inappropriate paint thickness.
Excessively-thinned paint.
Cheap canvas, very absorbent canvas.
Painting too fast.
Painting very small without proper brushes.
Aimless brushstrokes.
Faking it.
Showing off.
Working from photos taken by others.
Excessive glare on the canvas.
Changing conditions in the subject or movement of a model.
Deficient palette—poor selection of pigments.
Trying to paint what is not possible to paint.
Timidity and lack of confidence—fear of making a mistake.
Painting under excessive pressure or distraction.

Thoughts on Landscape Painting

Wobbly easel.

Not cleaning palette and brushes while working
Confusion—trying to do everything at once.
Trying to paint too much, especially detail.
Trying to paint what you don't want to paint.

There is nothing truer than truth. The mistakes committed by great artists are due to their having separated themselves from truth, believing that their imagination is stronger ... there is nothing stronger than nature. Sorolla 1915 Peel

The reality is that with a small amount of alteration almost any scene can be turned into a marvelous work.   Whisson

Every great mistake has a halfway moment, a split second when it can be recalled and perhaps remedied. Pearl S.Buck, Merriam-Webster

The man who makes no mistakes does not usually make anything. William Connor Magee, 1868, Merriam-Webster

If something bothers you in a picture, put it away and don't look at it for some time, and then take it out again and if it still bothers you change it, or you will never really feel easy about it. Rungius

Copying Others

VOLLARD: But how is a painter to learn his master, Monsieur Degas?
DEGAS: He should copy the masters and re-copy them, and after he has given every evidence of being a good copyist, he

might then reasonably be allowed to do a radish, perhaps, from Nature. Degas (1834-1917), Kendall

Thoughts on Landscape Painting

Too much time is spent in copying the works of others. And I do not hesitate to state also, that one risks spending too much time copying nature herself.   Meyer

How Long Do You Need to Look at a Work of Art to Get It? Scientists have determined that the exact amount of time one should look at a work of art in order to understand it is four minutes and eight seconds. OPA, Isaac Kaplan

Take every opportunity to visit as many art galleries as possible. On returning home, try to remember the work or works which appealed most. Flex the memory and make a thumbnail sketch - then revisit the gallery for a richer experience. Curtis

Without mindless imitation, don't be shy about stealing good ideas. Plagiarism is passing off someone's work as yours, but learning from their knowledge is an extension of their achievement. The caveat is that if you wish to study the works of another artist, make sure that he or she is competent. Watch out especially for the shortcomings of famous artists. Not everything they did was great art. They too had their bad days.   Schmid

The artist's interpretive vision would be lost in the cold reflection and recording of external facts. Reality is obtained not by copying but by interpreting.   OPA, Eli Cedrone

To be original one needs to learn the ideas of other painters in order to be different from them. Payne 1941

Don't paint as I do. Draw, draw, draw—that is everything. Sorolla 1915, Peel

Study books illustrating the work of professional artists, and try to work out what it is about a painting that appeals. In landscapes, look at the position chosen for the horizon, the shadows which define the form, and so on.   Attempt to imagine what the painting looked like in the early stages of production. Curtis

Thoughts on Landscape Painting

Be yourself. Do not emulate the work of other painters. It may take longer to develop your own style but you will go further. Denton

If you undertake to copy after one master today and after another one tomorrow, you will not acquire the style of either one or the other, and you will inevitably, through enthusiasm, become capricious, because each style will be distracting your mind. Cennini, 1435   Craig

The painter will produce pictures of little merit if he takes the works of others as his standard; but if he will apply himself to learn from the objects of nature he will produce good results. Da Vinci 1452–1519, MacCurdy

Immature artists imitate. Mature artists steal. Lionel Trilling, Merriam-Webster

Thoughts on Landscape Painting

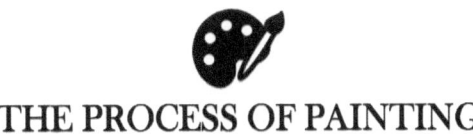

THE PROCESS OF PAINTING

Strategy

Tricks

Tricks are fun but they are not a substitute for professional skill. Schmid

Viewing the scene and canvas

Squinting

The purpose of squinting is to make judgments about the relationships among and between values, not to paint the actual shades you see during squinting.   Be careful of reflected lights within shadows. They are never as light or as colorful as they seem at a casual glance. Squint down at them, and you will see that they are about the same value as the overall shadow area. Schmid

It is very useful in evaluating the lights to squint or to close the sight with the eyelashes so that the lights are dimmed and seem painted in intersections.   Alberti 1436 Spencer
Simplify the scene in front of you by squinting at it. That cuts down the amount of light that enters your eye, and you see things in simple light and dark masses. I always tell people that artists have crow's feet around their eyes because they spend most of their life squinting.   Gruppe 1976
Squinting is not helpful in determining color. Colors darken when you do it, and you can't identify them properly. Open your eyes for color.   Schmid

Thoughts on Landscape Painting

The artist holding his thumb before his squinting eye. - measuring proportions - comparing relative values of the objects before him. His thumb has a constant value to compare them with.   Brown

I trust my eyes and the process of squinting to reveal the shapes. Smith

Never squint at your canvas.   People do this all the time because it seems to eliminate mistakes by making everything in their picture look soft and "arty." It is the same device that Hollywood uses to film aging movie stars (using a soft focus lens to obscure wrinkles). They only kid themselves and so will you. So to repeat—squint at your subject, but open your eyes to look at your painting!   Schmid

Standing and Viewing

It's best to paint standing up, if possible, in order to easily step back every few minutes and see what you've got going. Goerschner
Stand a good distance away from the canvas as you work, with your arm stretched out.   This way, you can see your painting and the scene simultaneously. Sitting down while painting may be comfortable, but it hinders you because you tend not to get up much once seated. You need to step back often to compare your canvas to the scene.   MacPherson

Walk backwards and forwards to alter your viewing distances from the painting.   Whisson

Seeing

A good technique is to practice zooming-in on just a part of the scene — that way you will not have too many elements to deal with, and very often the result will be a powerful painting. Whisson

Thoughts on Landscape Painting

You can't see everything at the same time. Your eyes can only see one part at any given moment. Therefore, draw by concentrating on one part at a time, but always compare that part against other things. Smuskiewicz

Check the painting yourself by viewing it over your shoulder through a mirror. This is a sure-fire way to see if the overall balance of the painting is correct. Trust your instincts. Whisson

Look more at your subject than you do at your work. The former will tell you where to proceed. The latter shows you only where you've been. Brown

To judge a color, look away from it to another object, and look out the corner of your eye. You should constantly move your eyes over every situation or scene, continually comparing values and colors. (Warm, cool, etc.) If I'm undecided about value, color or area, I work on another spot that seems to make more sense, then when I turn back to the troublesome area, I'm usually able to spot the problem. I find more often than not that these different objects in a painting have

something in common with other areas m the particular piece, and painting color and value too drastically usually results in the destruction of the whole. Be sure to train your critical eye on the painting itself, again continually moving from one area to another, developing the whole painting at once. Christensen

Think of your painting as abstract shapes. Look at it upside down If that helps. Brown

You must accustom yourself to seeing the ensemble in a flash and to rendering its character at once, but you also have to grow in strength and attack in a serious way bigger things with firm contours. It is good to draw everything, anything. You can't waste time drawing landscapes industriously. Pissarro, 1883, Protter

Thoughts on Landscape Painting

The surface on which the artist paints: an open window through which I view that which will be painted there. Alberti, Boorstin

"Knowing how to see" (Saper vedere)
He who loses his sight loses his view of the universe. Do you not see that the eye encompasses the beauty of the whole world?   Da Vinci, Boorstin

Conservation and Reserve

In battle, two things are usually required of the commander in chief: to make a good plan for his army and, secondly, to keep a strong reserve. Both of these are also obligatory upon the painter. To make a plan, thorough reconnaissance of the

country where the battle is to be fought, its fields, mountains, rivers, bridges, trees, flowers, its atmosphere all require and repay attentive observation from a special point of view.   So many colors on the hillside, each different in shadow and in sunlight, such brilliant reflections in the pool. In order to make this plan, the general must not only reconnoiter the battleground, he must also study the achievements of the great Captains of the past. He must bring the observations he has collected in the field into comparison with the treatment of similar incidents by famous chiefs. Not only is your observation of nature sensibly improved and developed, but also you look at the masterpieces of art with an analyzing eye.

But it is in the use and withholding of their reserves that the great commanders have generally excelled. After all, when once the last reserve has been thrown in, the commanders part is played. If that does not win the battle, he has nothing else to give. The event must be left to luck and the fighting troops. But these last, in the absence of high direction, are apt to get into sad confusion, all mixed together in a nasty mess, without order or plan and consequently without effect. Mere masses count no more. The largest brush, the brightest colours, cannot even make an impression.   The pictorial battlefield becomes a sea of mud

Thoughts on Landscape Painting

mercifully veiled in fog of war. It is evident there has been a serious defeat. Even though the general plunges in himself and emerges bespattered as he sometimes does, he will not retrieve the day.   Churchill, 1932

But remember, never make any plane so white that it cannot be made whiter. Alberti 1436 Spencer

Reserve is strength; overstatement is weakness. No one cares (as Emerson said) to hear the singer's topmost notes when the voice is "nigh onto breaking." This art of conservation is strength, and makes the masterpiece a masterpiece. Otherwise, the man who simply bought all the different colors obtainable, and squeezed them out upon the canvas to give it "full force", would be the greatest master, instead of being merely extravagant. Carlson 1928

I have a few "rules" for myself (which I interpret rather liberally). One of them is about subtlety. Whenever my composition is too obvious or overpowering, it interferes with my purpose. I want you to see my picture first, not my design.   Schmid

Resist the temptation to keep adding more details to the painting because the initial idea will go so far off track that the painting becomes irretrievable.   Whisson

Always try to conserve your values. That is, use as few different values as possible. You can put in subtle value differences later. The range of values is usually the first thing a student uses up. Make warm or cool color changes rather than value changes. Leffel

There is no better test of your colour tones being good, than your having made the white in your picture precious, and the black conspicuous. This effect you can only reach by general depth of middle tint, by absolutely refusing to allow any white to exist except where you need it, and by keeping the white itself subdued

Thoughts on Landscape Painting

by grey, except at a few points of chief lustre. John Ruskin - Elements 1857

Slow down for the hard parts. Slow down for the easy parts too. Painting is not a race. Savor what you are doing.   Schmid

Among the several characteristics of great treatment will be found reserve; the power which a great painter exercises over himself in fixing certain limits, either of force, of colour, or of quantity of work—limits which he will not transgress in any part of his picture, even though here and there a painful sense of incompletion may exist, under the fixed conditions, and might tempt an inferior workman to infringe them. It does not mean carrying it up to any constant and established degree of finish, but carrying the whole of it up to a degree determined upon.   John Ruskin - Painters I 1857

Blocking In

Block in the largest shapes first. Defining smaller shapes too early can fragment the image and make it difficult to create visual unity. Reynolds

Build up your picture from the broad masses; don't finish your trees, or your sky, or your distance first. Work on them all at the same time, keeping in tone like an orchestra. Keep them all in hand like a musical conductor. Have no false notes no discordant line or colour.   Sir Alfred East, from Landscape Painting Christensen

Start by painting large, flat color masses with your brush instead of drawing in the linear sense. This helps build your paintings simply and strongly from the start. Then work down towards the details, which are really just small shapes.   MacPherson

A picture should be laid-in as if one were looking at the subject I on a grey day, with no sunlight or clear-cut shadows. Fundamentally, lights and shadows do not exist. Every object

Thoughts on Landscape Painting

presents a color-mass, having different reflections on all sides.
Delacroix 1798-1863, Wellington

It's important to block in forms at the outset, keeping them very abstract. I don't even think of subject matter at this stage. Get at the essence of the composition: shapes and masses.
Goerschner

One of the great advantages of a lay-in by tone and general effect, without worrying about the details, is that you need to put in only those which are absolutely essential. Delacroix 1798-1863 Wellington

When laying in my design, I concentrate on the large light and dark masses. That shows me how the final picture will look. And it's easy to make corrections in the shapes of these masses while using thin washes; it's difficult after you've put down a lot of paint. As you work with these washes, try to fill in the grain of the canvas. Too much canvas showing through makes it hard to judge your values. A dark area, with spots of clean canvas in it, tends to look gray from a distance.   Gruppe 1976

Once the drawing is complete, I begin to average the color and value shifts within each mass and paint them as simply as possible. As I go, I decide whether color or value dominates each mass. If color is dominant, I use a narrower value range. If value dominates, I neutralize color. When all of the shapes are blocked in, I can compare them back and forth and decide whether the color and value relationships are in tune. Smith

I believe in a fairly complete oil lay-in prior to actually applying the color. I use a purple for this, since it's a lively color and will look good, even if some ends up showing through. Of course, some people like to block in their painting with earth colors-burnt sienna, for example. But a color like that is dead—there's no life to it. And it dulls all the colors you eventually run over it.
Gruppe 1976

Thoughts on Landscape Painting

I use warm red or brown earth colors for my block-in. Cool colors or yellows. Blue, green, and violet colors in an underpainting cause a "muddy" look when they show through the final paint. Schmid

Modeling Shapes and Details

When detail is added to your masses, keep it suppressed in the outer masses. Do not leave it out It is easier to centralize the interest in a composition with added light masses than with added darks. Carlson 1929

Many good pictures are ruined by constant striving to make them better. Over-modeling and accenting detail or highlights is an over-influence of realism. Payne 1941

I have a few "rules" for myself (which I interpret rather liberally). One of them is about subtlety. Whenever my composition is too obvious or overpowering, it interferes with my purpose. I want you to see my picture first, not my design. Schmid
Why embellish things gratuitously? Gauguin

Resist the temptation to keep adding more details to the painting because the initial idea will go so far off track that the painting becomes irretrievable. Whisson

Speed

Speed, is there anything more stupid? But, there is nothing that can be done without the patient collaboration of time.' Degas 1834-1917 Kendall

The rate at which you paint your picture corresponds to the time a viewer will spend looking at it. If you paint quickly, in a slapdash manner, the sensitive viewer will see a superficial picture and give it a superficial glance. Leffel

Thoughts on Landscape Painting

Learn to 'live' with the painting in the build-up stages: creativity is sometimes a long business involving constant adjustments and reappraisal. Curtis

Ideally, an impressionist landscape should take as long to paint as it takes to see. Knight

A painting cannot become so precious that your handling shows a sense of fatigue. Every faculty must be considered. The objective, although it may seem insurmountable, must be clearly seen and executed with certainty and complete confidence.   Christensen

Slow down for the hard parts. Slow down for the easy parts too. Painting is not a race. Savor what you are doing.   Work only as fast as accuracy will allow. Speed will come with experience. Besides, it is necessary only when the subject is changing fast, and even then a slow cool assessment of what is occurring, and careful paint application, are better than trying to frantically capture movement as it is happening.   Schmid

Painting a picture should be effortless and simple. If you work at a picture a long time, the picture may appear labored, lacking freshness and spontaneity,   Leffel

I have not found a correlation between the quality of the finished artwork and time spent executing it. Knight
As you begin work on canvas, start with a picture or impression in your mind and sketch. it in quickly. Then go back and do individual pieces. Leffel

Don't be in a hurry to produce a finished painting.   MacPherson

You must accustom yourself to seeing the ensemble in a flash and to rendering its character at once, but you also have to grow in strength and attack in a serious way bigger things with firm contours. It is good to draw everything, anything. You can't waste time drawing landscapes industriously. Pissarro

Thoughts on Landscape Painting

To finish something means complete, perfect and I'm forcing myself to work, but can't make any progress; looking for something, groping my way forward, but coming up with nothing very special, except to reach the point where I'm exhausted by it all. Monet, March 28,1893, Kendall

Fourteen paintings today, it's unprecedented. Monet, March 29,1893, Kendall

Studio Painting

In the studio, it becomes a whole different process. I typically work from field studies, and I'll set up all of my studies where I can see them. I might also refer to a slide, but just to rough in the contours. Then I'll turn the projector off and just use my field studies and visual memory for the color notes. Aspevig

Create a more ordered statement retaining the freshness of the pochade, but don't be afraid to let your studio painting take a new direction. Just as nature is a departure point for you to interpret in paint, so should the sketch be for the larger version. Don't try to copy stroke for stroke. MacPherson

I'm usually sure he's done most of his painting in the studio; that's where everything stands still. Gruppe 1976

Big easel pictures done in the studio tire me out and I spoil them. One needs to put into huge canvases all the fire and energy which are better reserved for murals. Delacroix 1798-1863 Wellington

It also helps to do studio paintings soon after plein air experiences, when the sense of place is fresh and familiar. Use the pochade for color notes and harmonies, taking more time indoors to compose, draw and design your canvas. Color harmonies and value relationships sometimes get off course when working with an outdoor study as reference, so use the same palette of colors. MacPherson

Thoughts on Landscape Painting

It has long been the opinion of painters that an hour's painting 'in the field' yields greater effectiveness than several hours of studio painting away from the subject, and I would whole-heartedly endorse this view.   Curtis

You must always keep working directly from nature. If you work too much in the studio, your colour gets too hot.   Rungius

First Things

Pick the easiest color to put down; that is, the easiest color to get right without a lot of mixing.   MacPherson

Establish your shadow pattern first, even though they will change rapidly outdoors. Painting the shadow shapes first is very important to assure clean bright color and a consistent pattern of light.   MacPherson
Start each new canvas with the idea of doing a beautiful painting and only secondly of learning to paint.   Leffel

It is easier to gain control over light family colors by first placing all the shadow shapes accurately. What are the shadow shapes?   MacPherson

Establish your lightest lights and darkest darks near the beginning. This will make it much easier to place the relative values between them.   Brown

The first piece of paint you put down is always correct. It doesn't become anything until you apply the piece of paint next to it. Relate the succeeding piece to the first. Each piece of paint should be a leading tone to the next.   Leffel
You can make it easier if you keep doing the simple, obvious things first. That way you are likely to get them right and they will help you to make the proper judgments about the more elusive shapes and colors.   Schmid

So what does one need to be a plein air artist like John Singer

Thoughts on Landscape Painting

Sargent?

Here are Carolus-Duran's methods for beginning a painting. (Sargent followed his methods).

1. Draw with charcoal.
2. Use a rigger, which is a round brush, dipped in pigment to state the masses.
3. No color or monochrome is allowed.
4. Shape, place, light is painted broadly in even tones of flesh tint like mosaic. No details.
5. No fusion of edges is allowed.
6. Make a tone for each step of gradation.

Philip Leslie Hale stated "Sargent never departed from Carolus-Duran's methods.

1. Wiping in darks were effective. He used unstudied shadows. (Does this mean he didn't put much details in his shadows?)
2. Putting in flat demi-teint. (demi-teint means half tone. A half tone is the color not in highlight or in shadow. It is the true color of the object.)
3. Cracking highlights into wet paint without bothering too much whether the value is right.   OPA

To ensure your background colors will still look good when the painting is finished, it's best to paint the background at the same time you paint the subject. Waiting until the subject is complete to fill in the background often ruins the painting because we tend to judge colors based on how they look next to other colors. If you paint the subject first, you're likely to choose colors that look good alongside the color of the canvas or paper as opposed to the colors of your background. Dawson

When do I paint? Always—I am painting now, while I am looking at you, and speaking to you. Sorolla 1915 Peel

Charles Hawthorne summed up the whole painting activity as "putting one spot of color next to another." Webb

Thoughts on Landscape Painting

Always work your backgrounds along with your foregrounds. A good habit worth acquiring.   Brown

Regardless of your subject, portrait, landscape, whatever, start by toning down that glaring blank surface in front of you.   Brown

Finishing

Getting away from your painting for a short period of time is good. Running away from it isn't.   Brown

Do not finish your work too much. An impression is not sufficiently durable for its first freshness to survive a belated search for infinite detail.   Gauguin 1923

One's eye becomes accustomed to details, when they are introduced gradually into one figure after another, and into all at the same sitting, and the picture never seems finished.   Delacroix 1798-1863 Wellington

Don't be in a hurry to produce a finished painting.   MacPherson

Knowing when I'm done is always difficult, so I just ask myself, "Have I accomplished what my original idea was"? When I think a painting is done, I set it aside and leave it for a week or so and look at it with a fresh eye. That's one of the advantages of being able to keep the paintings in the studio for a long period of time, instead of having to rush them out the door to meet a show deadline. I can come back and if there's something wrong or some area that's weak, it just immediately jumps out at me and I can fix the problem. Aspevig

Do not worry about finishing a piece, because it is how you start that is important, both for the painting and your growth as an artist. Finishing details will then progress easily and naturally. MacPherson

Then there are times when I think I'm only halfway through or two-thirds of the way through, but I feel like I could just leave the painting as is because it already says what I wanted it to say. I

Thoughts on Landscape Painting

never want to overwork something and go too far, but sometimes it takes guts to leave something without bringing it to an elaborate finish. Some of the best works are those that took the least amount of time and were left fairly fresh and unencumbered with unnecessary things.   Aspevig

Stop before you're finished. The best way not to overwork a painting done in the field is to stop when you think you are 80 per cent finished. You're really probably 90 per cent finished at that point. Put it away in your wet panel box until you're back home in your studio. Then give it a good long look and place those last ten or so brushstrokes exactly where the painting needs them. Goozee

A painter may finish minutely without imitating minutely; but he cannot imitate minutely without finishing minutely. Hamerton 1882.

When does a painting become art? Maurice Grosser said, "When it gets sold and starts on a career of its own." Webb

When you've finished the painting, take a break of about 30 minutes to relax. Whisson

Painting is a series of corrections; when there are no more to be done, you're finished.   MacPherson

If you finish like a photograph, on the other hand, the picture has as much personality as a photograph.   Gruppe 1976

When I think a picture is finished, I put it in another place, away from the subject on which it was based. The paint is still wet, palette and brushes are still handy. It is in a different light and on its own. I am no longer busy with matching some reality. The question now is how to make it better, stronger, more to the point, maybe even striking.   After all, it is destined to go out into the world all by itself.

Thoughts on Landscape Painting

First, I decide what the picture is really about and then what I can get rid of, what is not contributing to the central idea, what is distracting.

Second, I review the way space has been made to see if I can heighten the illusion.

Third, I check how attention is focused..

Fourth, and finally, I look for a situation or two where a couple of final, exquisitely deft strokes will convince everybody that I know what I'm doing.
                                                            Buechner

A picture (especially a light picture), if kept in a dark place for a long time (soon after it is painted), will sometimes "mellow" excessively; that is, it will appear slightly yellower when seen again in the light. In such a case, expose the picture for a day to strong light (not sunlight) in a north window, for instance, and it will be entirely purified and will never change again unless chemically impure colors were employed in its creation. The mellowing is usually the exudation of the linseed oil, or medium, to the surface of the paint. When a picture is kept in a dark place, it has no chance to bleach gradually as it is exuded. The above process is called "bleaching," and is a very valuable thing to remember.
Carlson 1929

When does a painting become art? Maurice Grosser said, "When it gets sold and starts on a career of its own." Webb

I work on all parts of my painting at once, improving it very gently until I find that the effect is complete.   Corot, Protter

Who ever thinks about Michael Angelo's work being finished? No great artist ever finished a picture or a statue. It is mercantile work that is finished, and finish is what the picture dealers cry for. Instead of covering the walls of his mansion with works of character, or, what is better, with those works of inspiration which

Thoughts on Landscape Painting

allure the mind to the regions of the unknown, he is apt to cover them with the sleek polish of lackadaisical sentiment, or the puerilities of impossible conditions.   Inness

I have a horror of something finished. Death is final. A revolver shot finishes off. The not completely achieved is life.   Picasso, Bell

Conciseness in art is a necessity and an elegance. The concise person makes one think; the verbose person bores. Always modify in the direction of brevity. Manet 1863, Gauss

Technical Aids

Photography

The photographer can change size relationships within the picture by changing the station point and changing the lens angle. Nevertheless, there is a certain tyranny of a photograph.   Most people believe it to be so factual that they wouldn't dream of changing its size relationships, value, colors, etc. Webb

Almost everyone does it. Even those who deny it have probably secretly given it a whirl. It was used by the Renaissance painters to refine their ideas on perspective, and there seems little doubt that Vermeer used some sort of projection device for his drawing. The 19th century Naturalist painters depended heavily on photos, and superstars such as Sargent, Sorolla, Zorn and others made free use of the camera.   ..... It is only a crutch when it is used as a substitute for skill or essential effort. Schmid

If facts were enough, you could take a photograph of the subject. Unlike the sensitive observer, however, the camera never selects or comments, never adds or subtracts. The scene is there, but the emotion and excitement are absent! Strisik

Thoughts on Landscape Painting

Step one: Choose a good photo
Step two: Play with the composition
Step three: Transfer the bones and lines of the drawing to the canvas.
Step four: Define the darks
Step five: Work the lights and mid-tones.
Step six: Keep focused on abstract designs and shapes, lights and darks.   OPA, Ann McMillan

Artists have used photography since about 1840: that is, almost from the time of its invention. As a way in which we obtain visual information, photographs are second only to direct observation. On some level, every artist is informed by photographs. Audette

Gauguin used photographs of Java, Egypt, and ancient Greece, and Degas (an amateur photographer himself) studied the stop-action photographs made by Eadweard Muybridge in the 1870's to understand how horses' legs really move. Audette

The Camera - I try never to be without one. It's an idea machine, it can stop the sun, freeze a flower, nail an expression. The camera is indiscriminate, but so is a brush; they are both splendid tools.   Buechner

Photographs are great for providing necessary information for bigger pieces, such as details or poses. Learn to read your photos. MacPherson

Work completed wholly on site, even after several visits, seems to engender more life than that completed with the aid of photography, where an unintentional tendency to tighten up the image can creep in. If, however, the painter has the experience and discipline of using photography merely as a minimum reference and can maintain those painterly strokes as on site, then the 'insurance policy' of the photograph can be of benefit. Curtis

Thoughts on Landscape Painting

Once you have developed a vision all your own, you will find that using a photographic image will be an aid to your personal vision. Handell

The collodion process would have afforded more abundant detail, but, to an artist, this additional detail is often of little consequence, being not the detail he wants. For the best photograph of any extensive scene never gives more than partial detail, however perfect as far as it goes. The artist, too, gives selected detail, that which seems to him the most needful and vitally expressive : and here, ten to one, if he is a good artist, he and the photograph will not be of the same opinion. Hamerton 1882.

From what I have said you might think I have no use for photographs. Far from it. They're necessary and practical. Even indispensable.   Brown

The details cannot be quite so accurately drawn as in the photograph, nor so minute, but there are more of them in the picture; and, in addition to this, we have the facts of colour and atmosphere, which have a great deal to do with our impression of any natural scene, and which it is consequently very desirable to preserve in a record of it. Hamerton 1882.

  Use your own photos whenever possible - If you took the photo, you'll remember the scene, if only minimally.   Approach your subject as if it were the real thing - Start with thumbnail sketches, value sketches, whatever it takes to become familiar with your subject — just as you would if you were working from life.   Create the center of interest. Your camera won't.   Beware of filled-in shadows - They're full of subtle color and detail — hardly ever the solid black they appear in photos. Remember, however, that you don't want to put detail in both shadow and light areas.   Brown

If you finish like a photograph, on the other hand, the picture has as much personality as a photograph.   Gruppe 1976

Thoughts on Landscape Painting

In a photograph of a view you see no more than a portion cut from a panorama; the edges are as interesting as the centre of the picture and you have to guess at the scene of which you are shown merely a fragment, apparently chosen at random. In such a fragment, the details have as much importance as the principal object and, more often than not, obstruct the view because they occur in the foreground. You need to make more concessions to faults of reproduction in photographs than in works of the imagination. Photography would be unbearable I if our eyes were as accurate as a magnifying glass; we should see | every leaf on a tree, every tile on a roof, and on each tile, the moss, the insects, etc. And what shall we say of the disturbing effects produced by actual perspective, especially where human figures are concerned? In a landscape, where parts of the foreground may be magnified out of all proportion without offending the eye of the beholder, the defect is less noticeable. The confirmed realist corrects this inflexible perspective which, because of its very accuracy, falsifies our view of objects.   Delacroix 1798-1863 Wellington

Simply duplicating, machine-like, what is in the photograph makes you little more than a high-priced enlarger!   Brown

The daguerreotype helps artists accomplish the reconciliation of true and aerial perspective and chiaroscuro with the splendor and dignity of elaborate detail.
Courageous, Ruskin, Boorstin

The camera cannot lie, but it can be an accessory to untruth.
Harold Evans, Merriam-Webster

Camera Obscura and Grids

This aesthetic aspect of "View of Delft" is directly linked to the image seen through the camera obscura which Vermeer was using. So his topographical view of Delft can even, to a certain degree, be termed abstract, as the optical phenomena associated

Thoughts on Landscape Painting

with this instrument - such as particular types of reflections and refractions and a lack of focus - are reproduced at several points. Vermeer 1632-1675 Schneider

I have often been struck, when looking at a camera-obscura on a dark day, with the exact resemblance the image bore to one of the finest pictures of the old masters.   John Ruskin – Painters I 1857

THE CLAUDE GLASS - This device, said to have been used by Claude Lorrain, was popular with landscape painters from the seventeenth century onwards, as it helped them to assess tonal contrasts in a scene. The glass consisted of a black convex mirror in which the reflection of a landscape could be viewed, the blackness modifying the colors to a series of tonal gradations - rather like a modern black-and-white photograph.   Craig

Here is a good aid for whoever wishes to make use of it. Nothing can be found, so I think, which is more useful than that veil which among my friends I call an intersection. It is a thin veil, finely woven, dyed whatever colour pleases you and with larger threads marking out as many parallels as you prefer. This veil I place between the eye and the thing seen, so the visual pyramid penetrates through the thinness of the veil. This veil can be of great use to you. Firstly, it always presents to you the same unchanged plane. Secondly, you will easily be able to constitute the limits of the outline and of the planes. Alberti 1436 Spencer

I hear what some may say, that the painter should not use these things, because even though they are great aids in painting well, they may perhaps be so made that he will soon be able to do nothing without them. I do not believe that infinite pains should be demanded of the painter, but paintings which appear in good relief and a good likeness of the subject should be expected. This I do not believe can ever be done without the use of the veil. Therefore, let us use this intersection, that is the veil, as we have said. Then, when a painter wishes to try his skill without the veil, he should note first the limits of objects within the parallels of the veil. Alberti 1436 Spencer

Thoughts on Landscape Painting

Take a Square Frame of Wood about one foot large, and on this make a little grate [network] of Threads, so that crossing one another they may fall into perfect Squares about a Dozen at least, then place [it] between your Eye and the Object, and by this grate imitate upon your Table [drawing surface] the true Posture it keeps, and this will prevent you from running into Errors. The more Work is to be [foreshortened the smaller are to he the Squares.   John Elsum, 1704 Craig

Mirrors

When you wish to see whether the general effect of your picture corresponds with that of the object represented after nature, take a mirror and set it so that it reflects the actual thing, and then compare the reflection with your picture, and consider carefully whether the subject of the two images is in conformity with both, studying especially the mirror. The mirror ought to be taken as a guide—that is, the flat mirror—for within its surface substances have many points of resemblance to a picture; namely, that you see the picture made upon one plane showing things which appear in relief, and the mirror upon one plane does the same. The picture is one single surface, and the mirror is the same.
Da Vinci 1452-1519 MacCurdy

Check the painting yourself by viewing it over your shoulder through a mirror. This is a sure-fire way to see if the overall balance of the painting is correct. Trust your instincts.   Whisson

Miscellaneous

One aid to judging colors accurately is to hold up something dark (like the side piece of my eye-glasses) over a dark shadow area. A thin brush or stick will do. This helps me see how dark, and what color dark, that shape is. Also, when painting outdoors, I often put a white tissue on a bush, so that I have a pure white object to compare colors with.   MacPherson

Thoughts on Landscape Painting

Look at a subject or a color painting through a blue or a red glass. This screens out most of the color and shows values. A black-and-white photo and a camcorder viewfinder also show values without hue. Webb

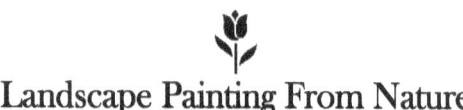

Landscape Painting From Nature

Philosophy

Never say plein air to me again! You know what I think of people who work out in the open. If I were the government I would have a special brigade of gendarmes to keep an eye on artists who paint landscapes from nature. Oh, I don't mean to kill anyone; just a little dose of bird-shot now and then as a warning. Degas 1834-1917 Kendall

Painting from life has been the most important avenue in my artistic growth. Many paintings done outdoors are a valuable source of information, an attempt to paint edges, tone, value, shape and color without any preconceptions or formulas. Christensen

The first element is the love of Nature, leading to the effort to observe and report her truly. No great school ever yet existed which had not for primal aim the representation of some natural fact as truly as possible. John Ruskin – Paths 1857

Immense numbers of essentially purposeless, semi-abstract pictures are turned out every year in the schools, pictures in which there is no real interest or involvement in the student's original subject Because it has been impressed on the student that he mustn't copy, whatever he does, his natural interest in what he sees around him is diminished; he feels that in order to be a real artist he has to 'make something out of it'. Dunstan

Thoughts on Landscape Painting

The artist always comes up against resistance from nature in the beginning, but if he really takes her seriously he will not be put off by that opposition, on the contrary, it is all the more incentive to win her over - at heart, nature and the honest draughtsman are as one. (Nature is most certainly 'intangible',' yet one must come to grips with her and do so with a firm hand.) and having wrestled and struggled with nature for some time now, I find her more yielding and submissive, not that I have got here yet, no one is further from thinking that than I am, but things are beginning to come more easily.   Van Gogh 1853-1890 De Leeuw

I never paint from nature. If I did, I would still be working on the same canvas.   Henry Miller   Webb

Nature does not capriciously scatter her secrets as golden gifts to lazy poets and luxurious darlings, but imposes tasks when she presents opportunities.   Payne 1941

Artists are now scattered, like leaves or thistle blossoms, over the whole face of the country, in pursuit of their annual study of nature and. necessary recreation. Some have gone to the far West, where Nature plays with the illimitable and grand—some have gone tropically mad. If such is the spirit and persistency of American Art, we may well promise ourselves good things in the future.   Van Gogh 1853-1890 De Leeuw

In painting outdoors, the first consideration should be: Does the view present a worthy motive? Is there quality that exhilarates and lifts the mind beyond the mere making of a picture? Payne 1941

A picture which is painted from nature, if well done, is sure to contain many truths which would have escaped the strongest memory in the studio, unless aided by memoranda as copious in detail as the very picture itself. Such works have, therefore, a peculiar value for their authenticity, independently of their intellectual or artistic value. When strictly topographical, they considerably exceed the most perfect photograph in interest and value as records of the scene they represent. Hamerton 1882.

Thoughts on Landscape Painting

Painting from nature undoubtedly weakens the memory and deadens the inventive faculty, and that to such an extent, that if persisted in without frequent alternation with studio work, or unless counteracted by the continual practice of drawing from the memory with the express object of preserving its power, the habit of painting from nature may deprive the artist of that faculty altogether.   Hamerton 1882.

A landscape is the portrait of a place. The face of the earth is an adequate and dignified inspiration for very great works of art. Sloan (1871-1951)
Do not paint too much after nature. Art is an abstraction; derive this abstraction from nature while dreaming before it, and think more of the creation which will result from nature. Paul Gauguin (1848-1903) Craig

If you don't work from life, life itself will pass you by. You need the experience of drawing from life to give your work conviction. Brown

With nature in front of us we can do everything well.   Sorolla 1915 Peel

The composition and design of a landscape do not come from copying the specifics of nature; it is more than that.   It is the power of art and invention which give pictorial beauty and strength of character to the works of a landscape artist. Alexander Cozens 1750 Meyer

Landscape is a living experience. It begins at dawn and goes through morning, afternoon, evening and ends in the moonlight. That's enough to keep anyone busy. Denton

Painting the truth doesn't mean making a literal picture of something; it means creating a faithful representation of an emotional experience. Strisik

Thoughts on Landscape Painting

You cannot paint a landscape without story-telling, for the mere indication of the hour of the day or of the season of the year will bring to mind the hours or the seasons preceding and following the hour or the season chosen. Cox (1856-1919)

I also hold that painting is essentially a concrete art and does not consist of anything but the representation of real and existing things. It is a completely physical language using for words all visible objects. An abstract object, one which is invisible, non-existent, is not of the domain of painting. Corbet 1855, Gauss

I proceed very slowly, nature showing herself to me as very complex; and the progress to be made [in understanding her] is endless. The real and stupendous study to be ventured is that of the diversity of nature's picture. Cezanne 1878, Gauss

There are painters who transform the sun to a yellow spot, but there are others who with the help of their art and their intelligence transform a yellow spot into sun. Picasso, Merriam-Webster

I've always had a horror of theories, and finally the only merit I have is to have painted directly from nature with the aim of conveying my impressions in front of the most fugitive effects, and it still upsets me that I was responsible for the name given to a group the majority of whom had nothing of the impressionist about them. Monet, 1926, Kendall

Landscape Subjects

Look at crumbling walls, glowing embers, clouds or mold, because in these irregular shapes one can find strange inventions just as we are apt to project words into the sound of church bells. da Vinci Audette

It is a curious fact that out-of-doors nature is to the beginner an enormously overloaded "property room". He sees for instance, the myriad of leaves upon a tree long before he sees the tree at all.   Carlson

Thoughts on Landscape Painting

The only thing I'd warn you against is the unusual or peculiar subject. Nature will probably look odd enough when you, get it down on canvas—don't make matters harder for yourself. Sunsets, for example, are too overpowering to paint—and they're impossible to live with.   Gruppe 1976

Don't paint "direct from nature" when all elements of organization and beauty or design are palpably absent.   Carlson 1929

Carlson suggested using convexity in mountains, trees and all natural forms. Concavity is reserved for ocean waves, snow drifts and hanging lines.   Webb

To make a good landscape you must sense and express the scale of things. A few rocks may be as important as a mountain range if you get a fine relationship between the texture of rocks and foliage and surrounding forms.   Sloan (1871-1951)

A common fault in the beginner is a tendency to paint trees which give the impression of stunted growth. It is a sound policy to allow a tree its full height and, if necessary, project the image to the top of the canvas, thus enhancing its majesty and presence. Curtis

Don't walk miles looking for a "subject", somebody else's subject. Look down the road and use your imagination. Get some excitement from the reality in front of you, the geometry of the forms. Get a kick out of the textures of materials.   Sloan (1871-1951)

Avoid pyramidal angles when designing mountains. Don't go up the mountain at thirty-five degrees and then down the other side at the same thirty-five degrees. Do not repeat the same angles on several mountains. It's boring. Webb

Choosing a subject is a very personal affair, but it always pays to seek out the right viewpoint at the right time of day. It can be so easy to go for the obvious, especially with commercial considerations in mind, having probably missed something close

Thoughts on Landscape Painting

at hand which might offer that little bit extra in terms of composition or content. The material with less immediate appeal can sometimes prove more enduring in the long run, and offer a unique quality lacking in the run-of-the-mill subject. Curtis

Observation

When trying to capture a strong feeling of light, exaggerate the reflected lights rather than the contrast between the highlights and shadows. That way, whether it's completed on location or in the studio, the painting will have the same glowing light quality that you experienced outdoors.   Smith

Repeat subjects for greater expression. The more intimately I know a place, the painted facts become less important than the truth of the whole experience. Paruch

Homer to Mr. John W. Beatty: "When I have selected a thing carefully, I paint it exactly as it appears." It is an illusion shared by other painters of our day.   Cox 1856-1919

Winslow Homer once commented in response to a tourist's query, "I paint exactly what I see." Homer was pulling our leg. Is it ever possible to paint exactly what one sees?" If Homer had said it straight, he would have said, "I paint what I want to see." Reid,

If in nature you come upon a scene that is naturally framed, you find yourself gazing first at one object and then at another and finally returning again to the first. In other words, you have found a scene worthy of becoming a picture. If, on the other hand, you find yourself turning to inspect the whole horizon, you have gone beyond the 60-degree arc that the eye encompasses, and have very definitely not found a picture. What you have found is a panorama. Poore

When a landscape is in front of my eyes and I am surrounded by trees and pleasant places my own landscape becomes heavy - too

Thoughts on Landscape Painting

much worked; possibly truer in details, but out of harmony with the subject.   Delacroix 1798-1863   Wellington

Even when we look at nature, our imagination constructs the picture; we do not see blades in a landscape, nor minute blemishes in the skin of a charming face. Our eyes are fortunately incapable of perceiving such infinitesimal details and only inform the mind what it needs to see. Again, the mind itself has a special task to perform without our knowledge; it does not take into account all that the eye offers, but connects the impressions it receives with others that have gone before, and depends for its enjoyment on conditions present at the time. This is so true, that the same view will not produce the same impression when seen from a different angle.   Delacroix 1798-1863   Wellington

The planes directly facing the sun are usually bleached out so most of the color lies in the half-tone or in the shadows. Anything that receives light will reflect its light into a lesser light. Outside, your shadows are filled with strong, reflected light and are higher keyed. Areas may appear very dark, but it's only because they are surrounded by strong, intense sunlight. They contain more color than you think.   McCaw

Several years before I went to Europe... I had begun to see that elaborateness in detail did not gain me meaning.... I could not sustain it everywhere and produce the sense of spaces and distances and with them that subjective mystery of nature with which wherever I went I was filled.   Inness

For me a landscape does not exist as a landscape, since its appearance changes at every moment; but it lives according to its surroundings, by the air and light, which constantly change. Monet, Boorstin

And those who paint 'em truest praise 'em most.   Joseph Addison 1672-1719, Oxford

Thoughts on Landscape Painting

Studies and Pochades

I ought to do some sketch-pictures in this way, so that they would have the freedom and boldness of rough drafts. Small pictures get on my nerves — they bore me. Delacroix 1798-1863   Wellington

Some artists paint important pictures from notebook sketches, put down "hot," that is, when the impression is fresh. These often convey more of the essence of the subject than the faithful "study" done at leisure. Poore

Sketch the same scene from different viewpoints.   Whisson

When I go on a painting trip, I usually take a whole lot of canvases in the same small size, perhaps 10 x 12" (25 x 31cm). I think they're easier to transport when they're all the same size. When I paint outside, I'm just trying to mix and match the colors and shapes I see. Aspevig

Can we expect from this almost accidental putting together of details that have no essential connection, that swift keen impression, that original sketch giving the impression of an ideal, which the artist is supposed to have glimpsed or fixed in the first moment of his inspiration? With the great masters, the sketch is no dream or remote vision; it is something much more than a collection of scarcely distinguishable outlines. A great painter concentrates the interest by suppressing details that are useless, offensive, or foolish; his mighty hand orders and prescribes, adding to or taking away from the objects in his pictures, and treating them as his own creatures; he ranges freely throughout his kingdom and gives you a feast of his own choosing, whereas, with a second-rate artist, you feel that he is master of nothing; he wields no authority over his accumulation of borrowed materials. Delacroix 1798-1863 Wellington

Unfortunately, it often happens that either the execution, or some difficulty, or even some quite minor consideration, causes one to deviate from the original intention. The first idea, the sketch —

Thoughts on Landscape Painting

the egg or embryo of the idea, so to speak — is nearly always far from complete; everything is there, if you like, but this everything has to be released, which simply means joining up the various parts. The precise quality that renders the sketch the highest expression of the idea is not the suppression of details, but their subordination to the great sweeping lines that come before everything else in making the impression. The greatest difficulty therefore, when it comes to tackling the picture, is this subordination of details "which, nevertheless, make up the composition and are the very warp and weft of the picture itself. Delacroix 1798-1863 Wellington

Everything is beautiful, the details, the whole. I would rather do nothing than do a rough sketch without having looked at anything.   Degas 1834-1917 Wellington

Never underestimate the benefits of thumbnail sketches. They help you solve big problems quickly.   Brown

The true method of study is to take small portions of scenes, and there to explore perfectly . . every object presented, and to define them with the carefulness of a topographer. . . . Young artists should never sketch but always study, and especially never make studio sketches.   Van Gogh 1855 De Leeuw

That's one reason it's often valuable to work on a small scale, to capture just the basic landscape elements. Further embellishments are best left for the studio. Strisik

When painting landscape in the mixed technique, it is best to make a small study in direct paint first. It gives you a memorandum of the color composition, with some color relationships inspired by the subject. Sometimes I make a drawing on the spot and work up the underpainting in my studio. I come back to the subject and glaze it from nature. If the underpainting is made out of doors with the idea of glazing in the studio, I make it in semi-neutrals and hues that will remind me of the color when I am away from the subject. I always make written

Thoughts on Landscape Painting

notations of the colors: the fundamental local color tones, the color-textures, and jot down some ideas for the use of color sequences—some prattle about my feeling for the scene.   Sloan (1871-1951)

Colored sketches, taken directly from nature, are the only means by which the artist, on his return, may reproduce the character of distant regions in the more elaborately finished pictures.   Van Gogh (1853-1890), De Leeuw

Dealing With the Sun

Keep the sunlight off your canvas. By using an umbrella to shield the sun or positioning the canvas in the shade, you are better able to judge your values and colors.   Cadwallader

Since the sun is constantly moving, establish a single direction and color for the sunlight in your painting. Keep sun-side (light family) shapes separate from shade (shadow family) shapes. MacPherson

When painting outdoors, you may find that the sun can be a problem. Avoid working directly in the sun as the brightness of sunlight makes it difficult to judge colors. Position yourself so sunlight does not directly strike the painting's surface. A wide-brimmed hat is always handy as it helps shade your eyes. Sometimes outdoor painters use a large umbrella with a long pole to hold it upright for shade.   Smuskiewicz

A painting done while bright sunlight is on the canvas will look very different when brought indoors. When painting in sunlight is unavoidable, at least try to have both your palette and canvas in the sun. (So the colors you mix on your palette will look the same on your picture.) Here is a little tip for outdoor painting, especially in sunlight—wear dark clothing. A white shirt will reflect on a canvas causing disturbing glare, particularly in the darker values of your work.   Schmid

Thoughts on Landscape Painting

If sunlight is present, it may be advisable to decide on a period of two to three hours for each visit and stick to this timescale until progress is complete. Curtis

When painting wear dark color top as light colors will reflect on your canvas. Do not wear red. John Budicin - workshop

Painting in bright sun causes two other problems (not to mention sunburn). First, the pupils of your eyes close down to pinpoints, which causes you to see less color. Second, the extreme brightness makes your mixtures appear much lighter in value. That, in turn, causes you to overcompensate by mixing your paints too dark in value. The result, when you see your work under ordinary light, will usually be a surprisingly dark painting. The simple solution is to have a big, well-anchored umbrella handy. Schmid

Probably the greatest challenge, however, is to paint directly into the light. Not only does this simplify form, it also challenges the artist towards effects no other light conditions can generate. The resulting appeal to the observer is immediate and stunning - dark areas are intense, while the purity of the lit areas has to be absolute. Curtis

Vantage Point

When approaching nature for depiction the primary consideration is the station point which will give the best translation of the motive. To get a proper view and idea of any subject, one should study it from several angles. The idea is to locate the easel at a point which will reveal desirable variations, not only of the size of masses but quality in line, values and color. Payne 1941

Don't work too long on one painting, on site. Ideally, about half-an-hour is sufficient to capture a light effect. If you work any longer, more often than not you will end up painting an entirely different scene to the one that first inspired you. Curtis

Thoughts on Landscape Painting

Push the center of interest away and place it into the painting within a setting. Then, to allow the first fifty yards or so, which should be the bottom foreground area of the canvas, to be used to lead the viewer's eye into the painting. This is a traditional approach to realistic landscape painting and it's a good approach. Handell

The location of the easel should be in a position where the shadowed parts and lighted areas will suggest the proper measures, that is, the unequal distribution of light and dark. It must be remembered, too, that shadows change rapidly and if the work is not completed in time, changing shadows may alter the entire arrangement. Payne 1941

Painting Outside

I recommend carrying a sandbag and rope with you. The weight of the sandbag helps to stabilize the easel against strong winds. A sandbag works great because you can fill it on location with dirt or rocks, then empty it and easily re-pack and carry it with your equipment. Cadwallader

Don't make a blue sky of gross blue and white paint. First, whatever the medium, lay down a pink or an ochre layer the same value as the intended blue. Then paint the blue into it for a luminous effect. Webb

Limit your on-site painting gear. Handell

Decide as to whether the sky or ground shall take precedence. Poore

Ideally, an impressionist landscape should take as long to paint as it takes to see. Knight

Probably the biggest problem with working outdoors comes when trying to mix the lights and highlights. Paint cannot reach the

Thoughts on Landscape Painting

intensity of light. You have to sacrifice some value to keep more intensity in your paint. As with so many things, you have to exaggerate.   McCaw

At noonday the landscape is just as fine, just as mysterious and just as significant as it is at twilight.   Henri 1923

It is needless to observe that no landscape can be painted from nature on such a scale, or with such a degree of finish, as would demand more than a very few weeks for its completion. The changes in local colour produced by the continual advance or decline of vegetation are so incessant and so great, that to paint longer than three or four weeks on one canvas, would generally involve the registering of inconsistent and contradictory facts, and consequently destroy the truth of the work. In the depth of winter, however, a longer time may be given and with a tent it is as easy to paint from nature in winter as in summer, except that the days are shorter. Hamerton 1882.

I have to stress the convex shapes of the earth.   Gruppe 1976

The fashionable landscape painters who imitated Claude developed an easy "recipe" for producing a pleasing painting:
Craig

The painter needs to be on the alert all the time, to perceive in the apparently confused reality around him the connections, the linking rhythms, the hinted-at shapes and balances which may bring his design to life. As one continues to work, to stare, pare, and make marks on the paper or canvas, one begins to see relationships which were invisible before, and which one s very well would be quite unnoticeable to someone who —merely glanced at the subject- even to someone who looked at it with love..   Dunstan

Thoughts on Landscape Painting

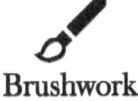

Brushwork

Brushes

Have the best materials available, especially brushes. You want a brush that will do exactly what you want it to do, instantly. Leffel

Don't paint from the fingers or wrist. Try the arm. Moreover, make some strokes from the whole torso. Lunge at your work as though you would tame a tiger. Webb

Two basic grips are used in oil painting: the pencil grip and the baton grip. Weber

Hold the brush well back from the ferrule so that it [and the hand) does not obscure the work. For much of the painting, hold the brush as one would a knife when buttering bread. Curtis

It works best for the most part to mix paint with the tip of your brush. If you get the entire body involved, the paint globs up around the ferrule, doesn't mix thoroughly and is difficult to control when you apply a stroke. Weber

Thoroughly mixing pigments and whatever medium you add yields a uniform color and consistency. When you apply the paint, you won't get any surprise unmixed colors popping up or drips of medium running down your canvas. The advantage to mixing pigments incompletely is that the color on the canvas is broken up by flecks of other hues, which can add a little shimmer and excitement to the paint body. Weber

Big shapes need big brushes. Retain your big shapes - use the largest brush you can. McCaw
A good deal of the time, you need to clean your brush between strokes and with the same motions shape the body and tip in preparation for making the kind of stroke you want. Weber

Thoughts on Landscape Painting

Painting at a brush-to-canvas angle steeper than 45 degrees evenly flattens out the paint, which is needed for smooth painting and blending techniques. Working at a shallow angle of 30 degrees or less is needed for thick brushstrokes. Shallow-angle application brings the entire brush body into contact with the surface, thus spreading the pressure over a much larger area.   Weber

What I want to do, is to spread good, fat paint thickly on to a brown or red canvas, and therefore what I must do to find a subject is to open some book capable of giving me inspiration, and then allow myself to be guided by my mood.   Delacroix 1798-1863 Wellington

Brushstrokes

A "mistake" done with a crisp, confident brushstroke will look better than something correct done with a flaccid brushstroke. Leffel

It is equally necessary to be absolute and decisive in your laying the colour. Either your ground must be laid firmly first and then your upper colour struck upon it in perfect form, for ever, thenceforward, unalterable ; or else the two colours must be individually put in their places, and led up to each other till they meet at their appointed border, equally, thence-forward, unchangeable.. If you once begin to slur, or change, or sketch, or try this way and that with your colour, it is all over with it and with you. John Ruskin - Elements 1857

With each paint application, with each stroke, do the "finished" picture. Otherwise, all those brushstrokes you weren't paying attention to will come back and haunt you. Leffel

> The anatomy of an Impressionist painting
>> There is uniform loading of paint surface —
>> even in the shadows.

Thoughts on Landscape Painting

Large strokes for foregrounds and small, almost imperceptible touches in the background.

There is uniform loading of paint surface — even in the shadows.

Introducing color into the shadows is important.

Strongly descriptive brushstrokes catch the character of the forms.

A sketchy execution is essential to the final appearance of immediacy.

There are passages of long unbroken strokes, short, horizontal daubs, and abrupt jabs.
Whisson

Brushstrokes should interlock and vary in size and direction. There is a beauty in an unmolested paint mark.   Webb

Getting Depth in Shadows. Keep shadows thin, so that no brushstrokes can be seen in the shadows. Impasto destroys the illusion of shadowiness. If necessary, use more medium to thin the paint. Leffel

Don't make your painting a long story. Brushstrokes are like words. One does well to remember that we are in fact picture makers or, as a friend aptly put it, we are visual poets. Knight

Beginners and mature artists alike should use more paint and more color. Leffel

Develop a variety of brushstrokes. If an artist uses the same brushstrokes throughout the painting the finished result will be a monotonous work. Use vertical, horizontal and cross-hatch

Thoughts on Landscape Painting

strokes. The key to an interesting painting is to use a combination of all these strokes.   Whisson

Nothing delights a student more than to draw with a paintbrush—the more minute the detail, the better. Avoid doing this. Instead, paint with your brush; think in terms of dimension. Instead of drawing individual hairs, for example, paint hair thickness or dimension; paint the light on the hair. Leffel
Avoid a too extreme contrast of size. One must be able to get all the sizes of the picture's marks in one focus. Webb

I like to work the paint like clay, as if I am modeling the object. Whisson

Give marks different lengths, widths and heights, and make varied size intervals between them. One interval should be crowned King. Webb

If too much canvas texture is visible through your paint, you will have a colored canvas, not a painting. Leffel

Vitality results from different size marks with strokes of various directions. Webb

There are two essential types of brushstrokes, one to create form, the other, direction. The stroke that goes along the form gives action and direction. The stroke that traverses or is painted across the form gives instant dimension. The choice of brushstroke should be part of the painting process. Leffel

Keep your strokes thin and true. Don't get thick too soon. It will gang up on you and become mush.   Brown
Expressing the theme with as few strokes as possible is the greater art.   Gruppe

A juicy brushstroke (one with lots of paint on it) makes an enormous difference in adding a dimensional quality to your painting. Leffel

Thoughts on Landscape Painting

A poet tries to say the most he can with as few words as possible. Similarly, the artist uses a few strokes— well-placed—to suggest a whole world.   Gruppe

Never do more than three strokes with the paint on your brush. Two strokes are better. Then pick up another batch of paint for each new series of brushstrokes. You can get rid of choppy brushstrokes in the background by taking a big brush and painting in one direction, horizontally. After you finish, take a dry brush, lay the flat side parallel to the canvas and brush lightly downward. Leffel

Keep away from the flat, overly-worked surface. You want to put down a nice load of blue and then pull orange over it. That way, the paint layers interact; one color mixes with another, creating "broken color"—strands of mixed and unmixed paint. In addition, the brushstrokes have a chance to register. When you see the stroke, you sense that the painter is working with authority; it looks as if he means what he's doing.   Gruppe

I try to keep my paintings fresh by not going over an area any more than I have to. If the value, color and shape are right the first time, I let those brushstrokes stand—right to the finish.   The freshest paintings are done with a minimum of brushstrokes in each area. I know it's an ideal, but try to lay it right down and leave it.   Goerschner

Painting is momentum. If you start in a half-hearted way with a slapdash brushstroke, it will be difficult to be enthusiastic later. If you don't begin well, you won't be able to decide when you're going to do it well. A marvelous painting does not evolve from 1,673 careless brushstrokes.   All art students should approach the canvas with serious intent. Always paint as intensely as you can. Don't wait until you're an experienced painter. Leffel

You'd be surprised at what the human eye will accept. Keep your shapes simple. Most people put enough strokes in one painting to do two or three!   Goerschner

Thoughts on Landscape Painting

Each brush stroke is a decision, and it's a decision not only aesthetically: will this look more beautiful?—it's a decision that has to do with one's gut: it's getting too heavy, too light. It has to do with one's sense of sensuality: the surface is getting too coarse, or not fine enough. I realize that whatever meaning that picture has is the accumulated meaning of ten thousand brush strokes, each one being decided as it was painted. Robert Motherwell Audette

It is possible to enhance the appearance of paint mixtures by avoiding the habit of overmixing. Colors that are mixed too thoroughly lack the brilliance of more loosely blended paint. When tiny pigment particles are slightly separated, individual brushstrokes take on a scintillation similar to impressionistic broken color painting. That is why it is a good idea to clean your palette often and mix fresh piles of paint frequently. Rinse your brush well between all strokes, and try not to go over them except to modify their edges.   Schmid

You can mix colors on your canvas as well as on your palette. Leffel

Oil painting tradition dictates that the colors be applied "fat over lean." This means that the early layers of paint are thinner and less flexible man those that follow. That's important: The thin layers dry more quickly, ensuring a solid foundation for the painting. The richer, juicier colors that follow take longer to dry. If this order of application were reversed, the upper layers would dry more quickly than the initial layers and would eventually crack as the lower layers move during the drying process. Iverson,

Since oils dry slowly, the more oils you add to each layer of paint, the longer each will take to dry. If you want to quicken your painting pace, you can experiment with a painting medium that speeds drying, such as an alkyd painting medium.   Brickler

Thoughts on Landscape Painting

The trick is to lay in the color changes with a minimum of paint (but never thinned) and resist the temptation to over-blend—one slow careful sleek brushstroke must do the job. The only concession to approximation I make is to sometimes (but not always) hold back on the thickness of my paint. Generally, I use my pigments spread thinly at first, using larger flat bristle brushes. Then when the block-in is finished, it is easy for me to go in and apply paint of any desired thickness (within reason) to achieve my textural effects. By keeping my paint to a minimum at first, I will have a choice of making those effects either very complex or quite simple. In working out the fine points, however, I have to be wary of losing the strength of the simple masses of the block-in. Schmid

Consistency Continuum
These paints have increasing amounts of medium, beginning with straight tube paint at the left. Their kitchen equivalents are listed beneath each consistency. Weber

> Margarine
> Peanut Butter
> Sour cream
> Mayonnaise
> Dijon mustard
> Ketchup
> Tomato sauce
> Cooking oil
> > Weber 2002

As you paint, don't scrub the paint into the canvas. Be sure your brush has plenty of paint, apply it, and let it stay. If necessary, you may push the paint around a bit, up, or in a curve, gently. There should be a layer of paint between the brush and the canvas. You might say the bristles never touch the surface. Leffel

One doesn't paint well by using a lot of paint, but in order to do a ground effectively or to get a sky bright, one must sometimes not spare the tube. Sometimes the subject calls for less paint,

Thoughts on Landscape Painting

sometimes the material, the nature of the subjects themselves, demands impasto.   Van Gogh (1853-1890) De Leeuw

Mix up thick, opaque color and put it down with simple strokes. The amount of paint on the brush, and proper brush pressure, is vital when applying your paint. Putting thick paint down boldly forces you to make definite decisions. Believe your first impression; if you look too long, your perception may change. Be decisive. A boldly applied stroke looks right because the artist made a decision and stuck with it. Putting down a stroke and then restating it once or twice pushes the paint into the underlayer, making the color muddy. Put it down and leave it alone. If the underpainting is too thick, scrape it off. You can lay paint over a thick area by painting the next layer even thicker.   MacPherson

When you paint, the brush should make no noise. Pick up enough paint so that it works silently. In other words, keep a layer of paint between the brush and the canvas. If you paint thinly, use enough medium to attain a silent brush.   Leffel

The natural consistency of oil paint is thick and butter-like. Its heaviness allows it to keep a good amount of surface texture, which can add to the aesthetic appearance of a painting. Smuskiewicz

Use more impasto, that is, thickly applied paint, where the center of interest lies. Impasto breaks the surface of the canvas and gives it more thrust. You can't get thrust without the impasto. It can also bring life to a dull color or area in your painting.   Leffel

The underpainting should be a positively sculptured low relief. I like to have the lights thick-but not too thickly painted, to give some "bite" to the glazes and to get a sense of texture in the light. Only by experience can you learn how dark in value the tones should be. Generally speaking what we call "pastel" is dark enough.   Sloan (1871-1951)

Thoughts on Landscape Painting

Mixing paint directly on the canvas instead of the palette is another way to achieve that casually mixed color effect.   Schmid

Paint broadly with heavy paint. Keep yourself from merely dabbing. Be more painterly. Leffel

To create thick texture, use a heavily charged brush. Put the paint down and leave it alone; let the brush leave its own special mark. When using texture to describe form, use thinner and more transparent paint to create the dark, cool shadows. Where dark shadows turn lighter, try introducing a small amount of warm color to the shadow mixture, instead of white. Resort to adding white (sparingly) only where the warm color doesn't lighten enough. Opaque, thick, roughly textured paint will lift the warmer, brighter lights. Zhang

Making use of the transparency of paint can also add immeasurably to the surface luster of a picture. I prefer to apply all of my darks very thinly when I can, particularly when those darks occur as shadow areas in the subject.   When they are employed together— transparently in darks, heavily opaque in the light areas—the three-dimensional effect is magnified. Applying darks thinly also eliminates the annoying glare of brushmarks in areas that ought to remain quiet.   Schmid

The brushstrokes must be spontaneous and direct. No tricks, you just have to pray to the God of all good, honest artists to come to your aid! Manet, 1987, Wilson-Bareau

Palette Knife

The first basic action used with a painting knife is spreading. One or more colors are picked up on the flat bottom side of a knife. A stroke is made by applying light pressure and gently lifting the forward edge of the knife's blade, spreading the thick paint out from beneath the flat blade. If two or more colors are picked up, a partial blending of colors takes place that gives vibrant color effects. Apply less pressure if a heavier layer of paint is desired

Thoughts on Landscape Painting

and more pressure to spread the color out thinly. A knife stroke can be used in several different directions to spread color out in interesting ways.   Smuskiewicz

The second basic action used with a painting knife is scraping. By holding the forward edge of the knife downward and firmly against the painting's surface, a forward stroke is made that lifts up the wet paint. This scraping action is similar to that of a snow plow. When scraping wet paint off a painting, some of the color remains embedded in the surface. This allows over-painting with a different color. If the scraped surface is painted into with a brush while it is still wet, some interesting effects can be achieved. Scraping can also soften edges or lessen the harshness of a color.   Smuskiewicz

I give you one caution—when you are applying paint with a knife, usually only one edge of your stroke will be satisfactory (unless you are lucky). That edge will most likely be the point where your blade touches the canvas first. Typically, the remaining edges will have to be modified with subsequent strokes with either a brush or knife.   Schmid

To paint with oils without using solvents, try painting alla prima with a painting knife. (Alla prima is a direct method of painting in which the work is completed in one sitting.) Using painting knives or bristle brushes, you can mix and apply the paint from the tube without solvents or a painting medium to thin the paint. Cleanup is also solvent-free; just wipe your knives clean with a paper towel.   Shesko

Thoughts on Landscape Painting

Materials

Oil Paint

"A most beautiful invention and a great convenience to the art of Painting, was the discovery of coloring in oil. The first inventor of it was John of Bruges in Flanders.
Vasari 1568 Craig

What a cursed medium oil is anyway! How is one to know the best canvas to use - rough, medium or fine? And as for the preparation, is white lead better, or glue? Should there be one layer, two, or three?'   Degas 1834-1917

Those who fussed and worried over paint costs were soon lifted out of their meticulousness on watching Sorolla treat paint like "so much mud   Sorolla 1915

Don't be afraid to put down thick paint. It's much easier to manipulate, and you can always scrape it off or apply thicker paint right on top of it. This layering of wet-into-wet color adds to the luscious overall look of the paint surface.   Macpherson,
Oil colors are ready to use right from the tube, but most artists prefer to thin the paint to a more brushable consistency with a painting medium made of a drying oil, a solvent and a varnish.
Walker
While many artists have heard the phrase "fat over lean," Raiselis claims that there's a good deal of misunderstanding about this principle. "It's not quite
as simple as it sounds," he explains. "It has nothing to do with thick paint over thin paint, which is a very common misconception. It's really about keeping the
underlayers mixed with less oil (leaner) and the upper layers mixed with more oil (fatter)." One method many artists use to conform to the principle of fat over lean is to mix in solvent for

Thoughts on Landscape Painting

the underpainting and to mix in oil only for the upper layers. The paint underneath the top layer should also be dry. Wooters

A GENERAL GUIDE TO ABSORBENCY RATES FOR COMMON PIGMENTS   Wooters

Colors With low Oil Absorbency (lean colors):	Colors With Medium Oil Absorbency:	Colors With High Oil Absorbency (fat colors):
Flake White	Titanium White	Lamp Black
Vermilion	Zinc White	Ivory Black
Naples Yellow	French Ultramarine	Alizarin Crimson
Chromium Oxide Green	Cadmiums	Rose Madder

Materials and Tools

Don't be afraid of your paints and tools. Be in charge.
Use the best available tools—especially when it comes to your brushes.   Schmid

Keep your palette orderly and clean it often as you work. Don't try to save leftover paint mixtures either. Glass palettes for the studio clean easily with a razor scraper and alcohol. Make sure your palette is large enough for generous mixing.   Schmid

Thoughts on Landscape Painting

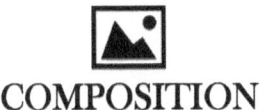

COMPOSITION

The Subject

Subject in Context

More often than not, the immediate appeal of a particular subject is governed by a special light effect at the time of viewing. It follows, therefore, that the same subject can have different degrees of appeal according to the changing light conditions. It is then the duty of the artist to search for that effect which so enhances the composition offered by the subject, that it makes the apparently ordinary subject appear extraordinary.
 Curtis

To ensure your background colors will still look good when the painting is finished, it's best to paint the background at the same time you paint the subject. Waiting until the subject is complete to fill in the background often ruins the painting because we tend to judge colors based on how they look next to other colors. If you paint the subject first, you're likely to choose colors that look good alongside the color of the canvas or paper as opposed to the colors of your background.
Dawson

Backgrounds function when they support the point of interest.   Goerschner

Choosing a Subject

Choosing a subject is a very personal affair, but it always pays to seek out the right viewpoint at the right time of day. It can be so easy to go for the obvious, especially with commercial considerations in mind, having probably missed something

Thoughts on Landscape Painting

close at hand which might offer that little bit extra in terms of composition or content. The material with less immediate appeal can sometimes prove more enduring in the long run, and offer a unique quality lacking in the run-of-the-mill subject. Curtis

Avoid the trite, the visual cliche. As Matisse said, "Ready-made images are for the eye what prejudices are for the mind." Webb

If in nature you come upon a scene that is naturally framed, you find yourself gazing first at one object and then at another and finally returning again to the first. In other words, you have found a scene worthy of becoming a picture. If, on the other hand, you find yourself turning to inspect the whole horizon, you have gone beyond the 6o-degree arc that the eye encompasses, and have very definitely not found a picture. What you have found is a panorama. Poore

When an artist is attracted to a particular subject, it is usually because of some visual reason—an unusual shape, an interesting line, an exciting color combination, or any number of reasons of this type. The specific attractions can be as varied as the number of artists painting their subjects. But knowing the reason for the attraction is important, because it is that inspiration that must be carried into the painting if it is to have life. Reid

In painting outdoors, the first consideration should be: Does the view present a worthy motive? Is there quality that exhilarates and lifts the mind beyond the mere making of a picture? Payne 1941
Paintings have no business dealing with anything either ugly or sad. Sorolla 1915 Peel
Pinpoint what it is about the scene that stopped you in your tracks. Whisson

Thoughts on Landscape Painting

In the initial enthusiasm of finding a subject that appeals, and being satisfied with the light source, it is easy not to use the placing of the elements that offer to best advantage. Curtis

Be careful about including words or numbers in your picture. They can unintentionally become a competing center of interest, stealing attention from where you want the viewer's eye to go.   Albert

Don't walk miles looking for a "subject", somebody else's subject. Look down the road and use your imagination. Get some excitement from the reality in front of you, the geometry of the forms. Get a kick out of the textures of materials. Sloan (1871-1951)

Ask yourself what made you choose your subject (just liking it is not enough). Try to identify the tangible (paintable) element, and be as specific as you can: Schmid

The painting has a better chance of working if there are fewer elements competing for attention.   Whisson

Unless you are excited about it, how in the world can you expect me to get excited about it?   Webb

People aren't interested in blueprints; they want to sense the painter's involvement and pleasure in the subject. Strisik

When observing colleagues at work, I have often witnessed a successful result emerging from a really vague subject in front of them - and certainly one which I wouldn't have chosen. The lesson is that what appeals to one painter doesn't necessarily work for another. Curtis

We must paint only what is important to us, must not respond to outside demands. They do not know what they want, or what we have to give.   Henri 1923

Thoughts on Landscape Painting

It is the ability to determine consciously what it is that interests him, and why, that differentiates the artist from the art student.   Carlson 1929

Your eyes don't tell you what to paint; your mind and feelings do. Anyone can describe things, but there's a magic to what the inspired painter does. That's what gives the artist's profession its dignity and its almost religious character.   Strisik

The student paints things, the mature artist paints ideas about things, or concepts.   Leffel

Interpreting the Subject

I am opposed to the idea that the subject of a picture is a mere starting point - a source of forms and colours, which may then be used/altered and varied quite arbitrarily at the will, or whim, of the painter This is an idea commonly held, and widely taught; and to my mind it is responsible for as much, or more feeble painting as the old recipe of exactly copying the subject.   Dunstan

An artist of great sensitivity and maturity can depart radically from his subject.   Dunstan

Do not have anything in your picture that doesn't explain itself.   Webb
A painter can either start with a subject, and let his composition develop out of what he finds in it; or he can begin with a formal idea which dominates the subject. This amounts to saying either "I like this sort of landscape, let's see how it will work out on a canvas', or 'I want to do a picture with such-and-such a relation of shapes'.   Dunstan

When choosing a subject I use my eye just like a zoom lens on a camera and I identify the most exciting aspect. I select a single focal point and do not paint everything I see because it

Thoughts on Landscape Painting

can be overwhelming; there's just too much to think about. Whisson

Augmenting the Subject

To make a good landscape you must sense and express the scale of things. A few rocks may be as important as a mountain range if you get a fine relationship between the texture of rocks and foliage and surrounding forms.   Sloan (1871-1951)

Adding a figure to a scene gives you the opportunity to solve composition and color problems. Figures liven up an area of foliage, they suggest mood, they serve as focal points and they give you the chance to add spots of complementary color and brilliant highlights. Figures suggest a story; they can be used to give a sense of drama, mystery or to transport us back to our carefree days of childhood.   Whisson

The conception of the subject is the important thing in art—that's the real measure of the painter.   Detail is merely additional entertainment—good for when the viewer looks more closely at your picture.   Strisik

The vastness of a scene is greatly strengthened by the presence of a lone figure. Poore

The inclusion of aspects of life and form once again require a good degree of drawing skill.   Figures, cars, boats. and so on make bold contributions to any painting and, if badly painted or introduced without a surety of touch could easily have the reverse effect, destroying the life and charm they might otherwise have created.   Curtis

Thoughts on Landscape Painting

Arrangement

Approach

The instant you make a mark on a surface such as a canvas or piece of paper, you create a "composition."   Schmid

Starting from his powerful memory-record of the mood and movement of the scene, he develops a complex formal design, but never alters arbitrarily for abstract or decorative effect.   Dunstan

Composition means, literally and simply, putting several things together, so as to make one thing out of them; the nature and goodness of which they all have a share in producing.   John Ruskin - Elements 1857

Usually any attempts to reconstruct, to a large degree, any composition after the process is far along will probably be unsatisfactory if not entirely disastrous.   Payne 1941

' Well composed '. Does that mean according to rule? No. Precisely the contrary. John Ruskin - Painters I 1857

The character of everything is best manifested by Contrast. Rest can only be enjoyed after labour; sound, to be heard clearly, must rise out of silence; light is exhibited by darkness, darkness by light; and so on in all things. Now in art every colour has an opponent colour, which, if brought near it, will relieve it more completely than any other; so, also, every form and line may be made more striking to the eye by an opponent form or line near them ; a curved line is set off by a straight one, a massy form by a slight one, and so on ; and in all good work nearly double the value, which any given colour or form would have uncombined, is given to each by contrast. John Ruskin - Elements 1857

Thoughts on Landscape Painting

The idea in any composing is to get the work to a sense of completion as soon as possible and then proceed with a feeling that the work may be left off at any time. As a matter of fact, many good pictures are ruined by constant striving to make them better. Over-modeling and accenting detail or highlights is an over-influence of realism.   Payne 1941

Regarding the painter who naively thinks that he is composing intuitively: It is a tragedy that one doesn't know what one doesn't know. Webb

On the whole, a painter does not consciously decide before he begins to do this and that; decisions are more likely to come out of the subject, his responses to it, and the way that other things are happening on his canvas. I am sure that pictures design themselves far more than we think; compositions happen all around us, and where a knowledge of these aspects of design can help is that it enables us to see and catch hold of possibilities that we might otherwise have been blind to.   Dunstan

Banging on a piano is expressive but doesn't make you a musician. Often times artists implement detail, bold strokes or skillful handling of paint, to disguise areas that are not understood. The result is artistic shortcoming.   Christensen

The painter who 'doesn't know anything about composition is still, inevitably, composing, when he sits down to paint even the simplest subject. He cannot put down one shape or line onto an empty canvas without creating a composition of sorts. But his very limited sense of placing and design is likely to be dominated by stereotyped ideas.   Dunstan

No law or formula can be concocted by which good composition would always be assured. I can only suggest that the student experiment with charcoal and paper (with any given motif in mind) until he feels that one arrangement out of the several made embodies his idea better than all the

Thoughts on Landscape Painting

others combined, and that he then try to decide why it is better. Carlson 1929

Composition, building up of harmony, is the fundamental process in all the fine arts. I hold that art should be approached through composition rather than through imitative drawing. Dow 1923

'Composition, tone, colour' – essential elements, considered in that order of priority. A well-composed subject layout can often stand up well enough to scrutiny, even though the subsequent application of paint may display limited technical ability. Without the core element of good composition, however, the result would not hang together at all convincingly, even with a moderate degree of expertise in the subsequent painting. Curtis

The compositional elements should be placed accurately so that the elements in the painting are balanced and the painting has a sense of natural grace. Whisson

Good paintings always exude an energy that flows from a harmonious balance of contrasts. Opposites pull and push, and the successful artist learns to control them to his or her advantage. Zhang

Compare the non-composer to the archer who, to be sure of hitting the target, shoots and calls whatever he hits the target. The most common reasons for poor work are: bad shapes, scattered or wimpy values, and no size dominance. It is better to deal with compositional problems at the outset than face the finished picture as an embalmer. Webb

Two main lines will start a composition, if they touch or cross. Every picture is a collection of units or items. Every part of the picture space has some attraction. Poore

In realistic painting, there are usually two visions, or images, that overlap each other. One is the image of the surface realism; the other is the image made up of the underlying

Thoughts on Landscape Painting

abstraction of the surface realism. These two images merge and are what makes up the strong realism and the design elements of the composition. With practice, they can be seen separately, but they are not really separate because they are continually interwoven and influencing each other.   Handell

PRINCIPLES OF COMPOSITION Dow 1923
In my experience these five have been sufficient:

> 1. OPPOSITION
> 2. TRANSITION
> 3. SUBORDINATION
> 4. REPETITION
> 5. SYMMETRY
>
> These names are given to five ways of creating harmony, all being dependent upon a great general principle, PROPORTION or GOOD SPACING. Dow 1923

Principles of Composition, I must repeat, are only ways of arranging lines and shapes; art is not produced by them unless they are used in combination with this general principle, — Good Spacing.   Dow 1923

A thing becomes "interesting" when it is well proportioned, possibly because all finely proportioned things function better than mis-proportioned ones, and we are interested in things that function well.   Carlson 1929

When there are many elements in a composition, a choice must be made about which one should prevail. If other elements compete for attention, simply emphasize the one you want, or subdue the others, or do both. It is easy to create a single powerful center of interest—just concentrate the brightest colors, sharpest edges, the most interesting drawing, and most contrasting values all in one spot!   Schmid

Thoughts on Landscape Painting

Composition is simply picking and choosing from among all the elements of the scene. I like to think of it as the placement of the big masses of the picture; you "compose" when you decide where to put the horizon, trees, buildings, and other elements of the painting. There are no hard-and-fast rules about placing these elements. I prefer to think of painting as a series of decisions, the exercising of personal taste, judgment, and discretion. Taste, not rules, is what gives a work of art its dignity, elegance and "tightness." Strisik

Shapes and Masses

Regardless of the subject, I reduce the scene to six or eight main shapes. If these shapes don't add up to a good abstract structure, I know that all the detail in the world won't save it.
Rohm

Nature may suggest shapes, but you must select the best shapes for your painting.
MacPherson

Focus on shapes, not things. Think of your paintings as mosaics of interlocking shapes; some larger, some smaller, but all related. Make all shapes interesting, and pay special attention to negative shapes. Start with flat silhouettes of color. MacPherson

The big form is difficult to preserve because by the time we have modeled the smaller forms upon the big and added the necessary highlights and shadows, the chances are that we have overdone these so that our big form is cut up and spotty. These highlights and shadows belong there, but we may put too many brilliant highlights upon it; meaning that we may put lights upon the upright form that should possibly belong to the flat-lying plane. This passion for putting too many and too brilliant "lights" upon all the forms or planes is responsible for more good studies coming to grief than ANY other cause.
Carlson 1929

Thoughts on Landscape Painting

In all good paintings it may also be observed that a broad simple organization of the masses and spaces is evident Even where there is much detail or variation, these do not disturb the bigness of the main designs.   Payne 1941

Reducing elements to the fewest and most basic shapes is very important in painting. Paint the big, obvious shapes and relation- ships; the little details will take care of themselves. MacPherson

Every good composition contains three or four main values. One of these masses is the darkest and one is the lightest, while others are near half tone or indicated with the intermediate shades. This does not necessarily mean that. Payne 1941

Mass is the other important pictorial influence that gives unity. Mass can combine many different objects that are similar in tonal value or color into one unit.   Smuskiewicz

A good shape is, or contains, an oblique. This means the edge of the shape, or more important its axis, is slanting in relation to the picture's border line. Shapes lurking parallel to the border are not exciting.   Webb

There is another way to group or hold together different aspects of a picture. If, at the beginning of a painting, some straight lines or divisions are randomly drawn across the picture rectangle in different directions, a guide is established to place things against. Parts or edges of different forms throughout the picture are placed on the same straight line. They relate to each other because they all are connected in some way to the same line. Whenever several different things in a picture share a common relationship, unity and control are established. Using rectangular line divisions helps to achieve this. Smuskiewicz

Thoughts on Landscape Painting

With regard to shapes, all shapes are in some way variations on circles, squares, or triangles. The variety of these shapes is endless. All are statements of potential interaction that could cause tension in themselves. Subjectively distorting selected shapes can add dynamic vitality to the composition.   Handell

A good shape is longer in one direction. Poor shapes have equal dimensions. Circles, squares and equilateral triangles are poor shapes. Because they are self-contained, they defy integration. The smallest shape is a dot. Despite its smallness, it be- comes assertive when isolated. A circular shape, though the simplest, is the worst for pictorial use. It lacks stimulation. Since circles in perspective are elliptical, they are less offensive. Almost as bad as circles are squares and equilateral tri- angles. These three shapes, having no direction, lack visual character despite their geometrical purity.
To avoid static shapes, stretch them out so each one goes some- where. Of course, it is absurd to stretch a shape so far that it be- comes worm-like.   Webb

A good shape interlocks with adjacent shapes in the manner of a jigsaw puzzle. Inter- locking holds the picture's parts together. Shapes should also inter- lock with the background. A poor shape is a shape that would roll if cut out and thrown on the floor.   Webb

Draw the big shapes first. Then divide them into smaller ones. Think large, then small.   Constantly look for opportunities to merge, consolidate and gather shapes together.   Make one shape larger than all the others.   Webb

Be aware that placing interesting shapes or elements at the edge of the composition could steal attention from the center of interest.   Reynolds

Shapes within a shape may be seen as values, colors or textures.   Make sure these are good shapes.   Webb

Thoughts on Landscape Painting

Carlson suggested using convexity in mountains, trees and all natural forms. Concavity is reserved for ocean waves, snow drifts and hanging lines.   Webb

First I evaluate the overall scene to make sure the big shapes can be identified, then I organize them into an interesting structure. Specifically, I try to visualize and break down the scene into three to five main shapes or masses. Detail is secondary to these shapes so I look past it.   Smith

As you draw, think of contour as a line between value shapes and not as an outline of an object.   Avoid tangents. Do not allow shapes to have a common border.   It confuses space. Avoid isolated shapes that do not consort with others. Use over- laps and configuration. Don't snob, hobnob.   Cross-fertilize shapes. Pretend the tree is a human figure or the cloud a bear. Such speculation may improve a shape. Feel the gesture of a shape. You are not only a spectator but a participant. Even a rock should have gesture. Try to feel the forces a rock "feels."   Webb

Because I group the similar areas in my scene by value or color and not according to the objects themselves, each resulting shape can include parts of several objects. For example, if there's a big contrast between the light side and the dark side of an object, the two sides each become part of two separate masses. At the same time, several smaller objects may make up one shape. This is what massing is all about. Smith

Avoid pyramidal angles when designing mountains. Don't go up the mountain at thirty-five degrees and then down the other side at the same thirty-five degrees. Do not repeat the same angles on several mountains. It's boring.   Webb

You have a tendency to use forms too round. Study Rubens . . . you'll see the power that is gained by slightly flattening the curves . . . It gives strength to a drawing. Wherever you can,

Thoughts on Landscape Painting

make up a curve of straight lines ... It is better to be a little more abrupt in the definite changes of plane. Rungius

To see strength, see your forms in flat planes — think of an apple unpeeled — a sphere made up of flat planes. Think of every round or cylindrical object that way. Tree trunks, for instance, rocks, boulders — make them so a single brushstroke makes the plane, to emphasize the plane and keep it distinct, make a light patch within the edges of the dark plane. Rungius

Focal Point and Center of Interest

Magnets for the viewer are of two types: a focal point and a center of interest. The focal point of a painting is the spot that attracts the eye of the viewer because it is visually appealing. The center of interest is the spot that attracts the mind of the viewer because it is intellectually appealing.   Albert

The focal point and the center of interest should be one and the same. In other words, the eye and the mind should be attracted to the same spot. If there are competing features, such as two focal points or two centers of interest attracting the mind, the viewer doesn't know where to look.   Albert

Try to keep your most vital and saturated color or color harmonies somewhere near the center of your design. If your arrangement of subject matter does not permit this, try to keep your most interesting or moving forms or lines near the center. (I do not here mean "center" literally, but somewhere away from the extreme edge of the picture.   Carlson 1929

Try to keep your most vital and saturated color or color harmonies somewhere near the center of your design. (Not the dead center) If your arrangement of subject matter does not permit this, try to keep your most interesting or moving forms or lines near the center. Carlson 1929

Thoughts on Landscape Painting

The center of interest is a magnet for the mind. It is where the viewer wants to look to find information. Two elements may be visually identical in terms of contrast or energy, but if one offers more meaning, that is where the viewer looks first. The best example of something in a picture that attracts the mind is a figure.   Albert

- Faces
- People
- Words & numbers
- Directional symbols
- Things in motion (runner, airplane)

Be careful about including words or numbers in your picture. They can unintentionally become a competing center of interest, stealing attention from where you want the viewer's eye to go.   Albert

Arrange the lines of your prominent masses in such a way as to point inward toward the center of the picture.   Carlson 1929

A focal point is a magnet for the eye. It is a feature in a composition that draws the viewer's eye to it.   The viewer will look first at any part of a painting that has these characteristics: Albert

- Contrast in tonal value
- Concentration of visual energy or detail
- Bright or intense color
- Hard edges
- Gap in a pattern
- Anomalies in a pattern
- Tangents
- Intersections or convergence

The focal point should be located in a place that is at a different distance from all four sides of the picture.   Albert

Thoughts on Landscape Painting

The rules of composition warn against placing something directly in the middle of a painting. And it's true that placing an object off-center makes the composition less formal and adds an immediate feeling of movement. But I've found that the center is a very powerful area that can be used for emphasis and formality. Centering an object makes an immediate statement about its importance.   Jones

The Rule of Thirds says to divide your picture into thirds vertically and horizontally. The intersections of the two horizontal dividing lines and the two vertical lines create what I call the four sweet spots. Any one of these intersections is a good location for the center of interest because each location is.   Albert

Watch for edges of planes or lines that exit at the corners of your composition. Always be aware of where you are leading the viewer's eye.   Reynolds

An alternate way to locate the center of interest is to divide the format into four equal quadrants. The center of each would be a good position for your primary subject. Either method will give you an interestingly off-center place to put the focal point.
Albert

"Visual traps" — lines, values, or shapes that meet at the same point (such as a tree, a road and the horizon)—can be detrimental to your composition. If your composition includes something with a strong perspective, such as a road, it's usually best not to show where the converging lines of perspective meet; otherwise, the viewer's eye is likely to follow the perspective path to a visual dead end at the vanishing point.   Reynolds

A unit of attraction in an otherwise empty space has more weight through isolation than when placed with other units.
Poore

Thoughts on Landscape Painting

Creating perfectly shaped "triangles" in the corners of your composition can draw the viewer's attention away from the center of interest. If triangles are unavoidable, soften the edges or stagger the form.   Reynolds

There must be one spot or area to which the other parts are subordinate and to which the eye is immediately attracted. This, the starting-point for viewing, must be simple and uncluttered and have the essential ingredient of leading the eye on further into the picture. Any one element that stops the eye so powerfully that it simply cannot go on is destructive to the composition, and must be carefully avoided.   Poore

Don't worry about where on a canvas to put your center of interest. There is no "right" place to put a center of interest other than where it looks best to you—where you hope your viewer will look. The idea that there is an ideal aesthetic center on your canvas is as silly as the right place for a cloud in the sky.   Schmid

In a pure landscape (that is, with no houses, people, animals, etc., to focus on), you have to clearly establish the point of interest with elements such as bright colors, high contrasts, sharp edges and pointing shapes.   Goerschner

Focal points are centers of interest—places you want your viewer to pay attention to—the vital spot where lines of direction and movement are supposed to lead. A center of interest makes good sense. The mind wanders when there is nothing to focus on. That's why politicians, art critics, and comedians are so boring (and why we often can't tell one from another). Having one dominant focal point certainly seems to be the best way to avoid confusing a viewer. Rembrandt, as we know, was very good at this, and his placement of a single illuminated face against a dark background is a classic standard.   Schmid

Thoughts on Landscape Painting

Start from a single focal point and work out from there. Make sure there is a lead-in to the focal point. Highlight the most exciting aspect.   Whisson

Commercial artists have a scheme for finding "aesthetic centers" by segmenting their picture with five horizontal and five vertical lines, then choosing a point where any second or third line intersects. Then there is the blindfold approach—drawing random lines, trusting in chaos theory to produce something. All such systems are a substitute for thinking, and in any case cannot be applied rationally to painting from life.   Schmid

Repetition

Shapes, or groups of shapes, may be echoed or 'rhymed' in different parts of the picture in so subtle a fashion that at first one can be unaware of any connection. In a landscape, for instance a small form can imitate a large and important counterpart; object; in the foreground can be linked in this way to others in the distance.   Dunstan
A single palm tree needs another with it (composite shape) to improve the shape and to establish a direction.   Webb

Repetition is the opposite of Subordination—the production of beauty by repeating the same lines in rhythmical order. The intervals may be equal, as in pattern, or unequal, as in landscape.   Dow 1923

Repetition is so fundamental a part of almost every form o design that it is rather difficult to know where to make a start Rhythm, whether in the musical or pictorial sense, obviously depends on repeating a shape or a direction, and the enjoyment o this is doubtless related to such a fundamental part of ourselves as our heartbeat or pulse. The repetition of an element in a picture can help to give a quality of unity, which enables the whole of complex design to 'hang together'. Repetition is not the same as repetitiveness.   Dunstan

Thoughts on Landscape Painting

Gradation

Whenever you lay on a mass of colour, be sure that however large it may be, or how- ever small, it shall be gradated. No colour exists in Nature under ordinary circumstances without gradation. If you do not see this, it is the fault of your inexperience. John Ruskin - Elements 1857

Gradate shapes from fat to thin, or vice versa. Typically, tree limbs get thinner as they become more distant from the trunk. Shape gradation can be initiated in negative shapes if positives are tilted.   Webb

Space without detail may possess attraction by gradation and by suggestion. Poore

Two straight lines meeting in opposing directions give an impression of abruptness, severity, or even violence ; the difference of movement being emphasized. If a third line is added, as in the sketches below, the opposition is softened and an effect of unity and completeness produced.   Dow 1923

Line

Just as the vertical may be called the figure painter's line, the horizontal is the landscape painter's line. Poore

Placing two important lines or directions so that they would meet at a right-angle if extended is one of the oldest and most universally-used ways of strengthening the design of a picture- it has the effect of locking it together, one might say. You will very often find this device used by Degas, who was master of logical and deliberate composition; a master, too, of the use of diagonal movements and thrusts, which is implicit in this type of design.   Dunstan

Two lines meeting form a simple and severe harmony.   Dow 1923

Thoughts on Landscape Painting

Try to establish at least one vertical and one horizontal, and their relationship within the limits of the canvas. Curtis

Avoid tangents. Instead make a decisive overlap. Stop and detour any line straying to a corner. Use lines to slow up or stop other main lines that are approaching the picture border. Is a contour line really needed at a value edge? Avoid line when color-value shapes read clearly. If you have a ragged or sawtooth line, oppose it with a simple, un- eventful line. For example, the far shoreline of a lake is straight and simple, whereas the near shoreline is full of incident. Relate line (edge) to value. Flat values are best expressed with straight line. Highly modeled value shapes, like clouds, call for undulating contour. Webb

Always have one longest line whether straight or curved. It adds backbone. Create junction at the center of interest. Use lines to lead the eye there. If your scheme is mostly curves, introduce some straights, not only for variety's sake, but also to relate to the border. Webb

One simple but important effect of line is how it gives borders or edges to forms, enclosing them and defining what the forms are made of. Another important function of line is to give direction and lead the viewer through a picture. Sometimes lines are strong divisions between different tonal and color areas. At other times, linear edges of several individual forms can combine to form a single strong line. This line not only helps carry the viewer's glance along it but it can also hold together a picture's many disparate parts. Smuskiewicz

Scribble gestures. Feel the action of the opposing directions. Visualize the hidden linear axis in every volume you draw. Sense your border lines as you put down other lines. They affect the lines of your subject. Think of lines not as the

Thoughts on Landscape Painting

edges of objects but as the boundaries of two value shapes. Webb

Any long line (edge) should have incident en route. A value, color, cross-line or other interrupter should be provided to create pause or relief and to integrate the long line. This incident generally will be a value change, color change, or line which passes behind the long line at a good place; not at the center and not too near one end.   Webb

They say there is no straight line in nature. This is a lie like all that they say, for there is every line in nature. But I will tell them what there is not in nature. An even tint is not in nature—it produces heaviness. Nature's shadows are ever varying, and a ruled sky. Blake, Protter

Simplification

"Keep it simple" applies to just about every aspect of painting: gear, subject matter, painting process, colors, etc. MacPherson

Simplification is obviously necessary before you can paint many of the things you see. Schmid
Do everything the simplest way you can.   Leffel

Simplicity is one of the key elements of good composition. You have to learn to see the landscape in terms of a few large patterns. The eye naturally craves such ordering principles. Strisik

Commandment to the beginner—Select simple arrangements. Payne 1941

Simple ideas are what good paintings are all about; the complexity is in the choice of values color changes, arrangement drawing, surface variety, edges, etc. So you ask yourself, "How much more can a painting bear and be effective? Putting more into a painting can be wonderful, (with sensitive juxtapositions, etc.) presupposing everything is m harmony or academically correct up to that point. But the question is -" Can the additional things added aid in the solidarity? Can the Painting remain firm under such a load?" If the load is light, maybe! And how will this affect the main idea of our picture? These are critical questions you should ask yourself while painting. These are the things that separate one painter from another: their temperament if you will. Christensen

When faced with such a distractingly complicated scene, I must first of all choose a typical incident and define my picture, as if I could already see it framed. Manet, 1987, Wilson-Barea

Balance

The challenge for the artist becomes one of finding the right dynamic balance each time the easel is set up outside: to observe, perceive, interpret and abstract   Knight

The term Symmetry applies to three and four-part groups, or others where even balance is made, but here it refers mainly to a two-part arrangement.   Dow 1923

In varying degrees, pictures express what may be termed a natural axis, an axis on which the picture components are arranged in a balanced composition.   Balance across the middle creates unity in the picture, limiting it within its frame. We can see it easily where the subject has little depth of background. Poore

I try for slight imbalance in my paintings, that is, the painting is not perfectly balanced but rather has an energy tike a set of scales attempting to gain balance. Knight

Thoughts on Landscape Painting

Unity and Variety

The great aim of composition is to create unity and that ONE feature should be the interest and dominate all other interests or masses. Practically all other writers on art agree that this is the main principle in creating unified designs.   Payne 1941

The great object of composition being always to secure unity ; that is, to make out of many things one whole ; the first mode in which this can be effected is, by determining that one feature shall be more important than all the rest, and that the others shall group with it in subordinate positions.   John Ruskin - Elements 1857

Another important and pleasurable way of expressing unity, is by giving some orderly succession to a number of objects more or less similar. And this succession is most interesting when it is connected with some gradual change in the aspect or character of the objects. Thus the succession of the pillars of a cathedral aisle is most interesting.   John Ruskin - Elements 1857

Deciding the unequal quantity or measure of masses, spaces, color, values and their placement, establishing the horizon and other main lines, and creating artistic equalization in perspective or recession are the chief principles of full balance in all directions.   Payne 1941

An important means of expressing unity is to mark some kind of sympathy among the different objects, and perhaps the pleasantest, because most surprising, kind of sympathy, is when one group imitates or repeats another; not in the way of balance or symmetry, but subordinately, like a far-away and broken echo of it.   John Ruskin - Elements 1857

Break lines into different measures — some short, some middle- sized, and some long. On curves use different size radii—some slow curves and some fast ones.   Webb

Unity is necessary because without it our minds and eyes are worried by disorganized muddle. Some shape and pattern has to be imposed; things have to 'hang together'. On the other hand, without variety, our second need, our eyes quickly become bored and lose interest.   Dunstan

Never make any two intervals the same.   Albert

Do not divide your canvas into equal-sized spaces unless you do so for a definite artistic reason.   Carlson 1929

Ruskin says, in as many words, that the great aim of composition is to create unity and that one feature should be the main interest and dominate all other interests or masses. Practically all other writers on art agree that this is the main principle in creating unified designs.   Payne 1941

A good painting has unity and variety. Variety adds interest. Design your shapes to add variety. Create each major shape differently. Think of your painting a mosaic of large and small interlocking shapes. Do not paint things. The correct shapes and color notes in the right places create realistic images. MacPherson

Ensure objects have variety in shape, size and distance apart. Whisson

Avoid duplicating the direction of your main line. It's usually better to make opposing lines. • Negative shapes also require varied directions. Webb

Edges around a shape need variety. There are only three kinds of edge: hard, soft, and rough. The best shapes use all three. Avoid Parallel Edges.   Webb

Dividing a composition into equal parts horizontally or vertically can lead to a static composition.   Dividing your

Thoughts on Landscape Painting

design into too many similar shapes is apt to produce an uninteresting painting. Likewise, be sure the negative spaces between objects aren't all the same width or height. Reynolds

Create each major shape differently. Think of your painting a mosaic of large and small interlocking shapes. Do not paint things. The correct shapes and color notes in the right places create realistic images.   MacPherson

The principle Subordination is a great constructive idea not only in the space arts but in all the fine arts: To form a complete group the parts are attached or related to a single dominating element which determines the character of the whole.   Dow 1923

In painting any view, the artist must concentrate his powers to unify the work. Otherwise it will not bear the peculiar imprint of his soul. ... If a painter forces himself to work when he feels lazy his productions will be weak and spiritless, without precision. Kuo Hsi, Boorstin

Nature abhors a vacuum, say the physicists. They should complete their axiom by adding that it has no less a horror of regularity. Renoir 1884, Gauss

Golden Section

The Golden Section is a perfect ratio of approximately 1.618 to one or, conversely, one to .618.   The closest general fraction in five to eight or 5/8.   Nordquist

The use of the upper Golden Section - one- third down from the upper horizontal edge — means that greater attention and importance will be given to the land mass. Herein lies one of the great fears of the student painter - the inevitable inclusion of a considerable area of foreground content much of which,

Thoughts on Landscape Painting

on the face of it, may not offer a great deal in the way of interest.   Curtis

So the way that the picture rectangle is divided, vertically and horizontally, is likely to be an important factor in the design ol many different types of picture. The Golden Section system can be summed up as a way of making-divisions and sub-divisions of a line or a rectangle without ever repeating yourself.   Dunstan

Drawing

Draw, draw, draw—that is everything. Sorolla 1915 Peel

A drawing badly started takes on the same misbegotten authority as a false printed word.   Webb

Good drawing is, as we have seen, an abstract of natural facts ; you cannot represent all that you would, but must continually be falling short, whether you will or no, of the force, or quantity, of Nature.   John Ruskin - Elements 1857

You can't see everything at the same time. Your eyes can only see one part at any given moment. Therefore, draw by concentrating on one part at a time, but always compare that part against other things.   Smuskiewicz

The outlines of contours present problems for many artists, particularly in figure or portrait painting. Here are some things to think about: Most curves are rarely as "curvy" as they first appear, and inexperienced artists usually exaggerate them. The way to get around curves (pardon the pun) is to think of every curve as a series of straight lines that change direction. If you paint them with that in mind, they will be stronger, more interesting, and far more accurate than a single nondescript curve.   Schmid

Thoughts on Landscape Painting

Measure twice, draw once.   Believe your eye. But trust measurements.   Brown

Start with charcoal rather than paint.   Gruppe 1976

Study the silhouette of every object; distinctness of outline is the attribute of the hand that is not enfeebled by any hesitation of the will. Gauguin (1848-1903)

Sketch the same scene from different viewpoints.   Whisson

No law or formula can be concocted by which good composition would always be assured. I can only suggest that the student experiment with charcoal and paper (with any given motif in mind) until he feels that one arrangement out of the several made embodies his idea better than all the others combined, and that he then try to decide why it is better. Carlson 1929

Texture

Texture can differentiate parts of a painting, though value and color are more effective. Since we "see" with the sense of touch as much as with the eye, use softness, roughness, wetness and dryness to give validity to certain areas.   Too much textural contrast in a painting produces disunity. Beware of extreme smoothness in one area and high impasto in other areas. Extreme brightness will tend to make texture invisible. Therefore, if you wish a light value to take on a luminous look, eliminate texture. The textures of nature are a given and every surface has one. The painter needs to sense these, but more important you need to seek out and allocate texture with positive intention and not merely copy nature's texture. Webb

Thoughts on Landscape Painting

Perspective

Perspective as it concerns Painting is divided into three chief parts of which the first treats of the diminution in the size of bodies at different distances. The second is that which treats of the diminution it the color of these bodies. The third of the gradual loss of distinction of the forms and outlines of these bodies at various distances.   Da Vinci 1452-1519 MacCurdy

Near always means more—more color, stronger value, sharper edges, more contrast. Leffel

It is also advisable to go some distance away, because then the work appears smaller, and more of it is taken in at a glance, and a lack of harmony or proportion in the various parts and in the colours of the objects is more readily seen.   Da Vinci 1452-1519 MacCurdy

Leading lines should carry the eye into the picture or towards the subject. Poore
Where any sequence of similar or regular forms occurs, arrange the forms in such a way as to diminish in size toward the inside of your canvas rather than the reverse, thereby strengthening the suggestion of depth, or recession of space, in the canvas.   Carlson 1929

As painted images recede into the distance, textures should be eliminated. Webb

Warm colors advance and cool colors recede. The human eye expresses a natural preference for yellow, red, orange; it sees gray, blue, green only peripherally.   Leffel 1995

All colours in distant shadows are indistinguishable and indiscernible.   Da Vinci 1452-1519 MacCurdy

Darks get lighter as they go further back. Light is more constant outdoors as well as indoors. Leffel

Thoughts on Landscape Painting

But in the far distance that object will show itself most blue which is darkest in colour. Da Vinci 1452-1519 MacCurdy

When something goes back into space, its value should be similar to other values in the same plane so that it won't stand out. There should be a close relationship. When something comes forward, there should be less of a relationship with its background and more of a contrast of values.   Leffel

Visual Movement

Visual Movement Theory

When reverie begins in a picture, the eye involuntarily makes a circuit of the items presented, starting at the most interesting and widening towards the circumference, as ring follows ring when a stone is thrown into water. Poore
When a child learns to read, he learns to start at the upper left of the page and moves down toward the right. The upper-left corner then is a good entry point for the viewer. Albert

The eye will tend to follow certain directions more readily than others. The simplest example of this is our tendency to 'read' a picture from left to right, in the same way that you are reading this page.   Dunstan

Lines of Motion

Of two lines of equal force the vertical is the one first seen. In composition, therefore, it takes precedence. Poore

Verticals divide, horizontals expand. Leffel

Just as the vertical may be called the figure painter's line, the horizontal is the landscape painter's line. Poore

Thoughts on Landscape Painting

Directing the viewer's attention as she scans your picture is part of your job as an artist. You can control what the viewer sees and when the viewer sees it. You also want to keep the viewer's attention freely circulating. You can accomplish both by the use of lines, leads and pointers which direct the eye to where you want it to go, and by avoiding leaks that allow it to escape. You want to provide a clear visual trail for the eye to follow through the picture. Lines, leads and pointers form the path of least resistance, naturally attracting a viewer's attention. Any linear element in a picture, such as a line or long, narrow shape, will create a path for the eye to follow. An arrow-like shape can act as a pointer, too, directing the eye to wherever it points. These devices can lead the eye out of the picture as well as into it, so you need to be aware of their affect on the viewer's attention.   Albert

The experimenting with lines which carry the eye away from the focal point and lead it through the picture—a groping for an item, an accent, or something that will attract the eye away from the corner or side of the picture, where, in following the leading lines, it may be brought back towards the focus again. Poore

When composing in slanting directions, include some verticals and horizontals. This not only gives variety but stabilizes the exuberance and keys the picture to its frame. Webb

When using converging lines, be careful you aren't "capturing" the viewer's eye and preventing it from moving through the painting.   Reynolds

Use directional lines to lead the eye to this main focal point and subtle lines lead away from the focal point to a secondary point.   Whisson

LINES OF DIRECTION are the conspicuous edges of shapes (or actual lines) in a painting that presumably "lead" an

Thoughts on Landscape Painting

observer's eye elsewhere. Some subjects have them, other don't. Some subjects have no strong lines at all, and that's fine. Lines are not the only tools we have. MOVEMENT and RHYTHM are also assumptions about controlling the attention of an observer's eye except that shapes are involved instead of lines. Movement can probably best be described as the use of more or less connected shapes to nudge a viewer's interest around within a painting-stopping at the main dish, of course-then going around again.
Rhythm is the repetition of certain similar shapes intended to make things more pleasant along the way.... Schmid

Only when the force of these horizontals is broken, either by the sky or by zigzag, angular forms, can the eye come to rest on the subject itself. A great danger of long lines—which are so attractive to the eye—is that they can very easily lead the eye away from the subject and right out of the picture. Poore

Getting out of the picture successfully is every bit as important as getting into it. This does not mean, however, backing out. Passing through and out is the main objective, but you must create the exit you want. This means avoiding at all costs possible escapes en route and providing a single logical means of leaving the picture. Poore

Curved lines contribute more to rhythmic feeling than any other type of line. Yet curved line generally needs opposition by a least a few straight lines. A predominance of curved or slanting lines might have a great degree of movement, yet there is such a thing as too much. Some upright and lateral straight lines are usually needed in such an instance to slow the too speedy glance. Payne 1941

Just as we enter the picture by means of curves or zigzags, we should leave the same way. The eye should never be permitted to leave the principal figure or object and go straight back and out through the middle. If this is allowed, the width of the picture is neglected. Therefore, if the

Thoughts on Landscape Painting

attraction of the natural exit is greater than other objects, there is no valid reason for their existence. Poore

It is through a feeling of design and 'lead-in' that one can use the space to great advantage; a typical example would be the leading of the eye along a twisting pathway up to some dramatic point of interest. Furthermore, the ability to resolve foreground areas in close-toned blocks or asses, and to go for sweeping shadow areas and he inclusion of figurative interest, will all enable he painter to increase the features of interest. Curtis

The subjective use of directional lines can also create a sense of compositional tension. The same is true with color, values, textures, or any of the compositional elements. In a sense, tension can be defined as the attraction, repulsion, and interaction of the diverse compositional elements. Varying degrees of compositional tension can be built into a painting by choice, inter-weaving the elements of the painting in a balanced, tightly knit manner.   Handell

By varying the lines in your picture, you can give it added life. In his still lifes, Cezanne always slanted the table so that it angled into the picture, drawing the viewer in and avoiding lines that parallel the frame. He also looked down on his subject, further emphasizing the leading diagonal lines. You can use his ideas in your own outdoor work. Just remember that perfectly straight lines are boring-look for the diagonals! They give your picture variety and vitality.   Gruppe 1976

Movement is energy. It is integral to composition. It can be the backbone of certain compositions or it could quietly weave through a composition. Movement in a composition determines how the viewer's eye travels into, through, and around a painting.   Handell

Eye movements are guided primarily by shapes directing the viewer's attention to the point of interest. Then these shapes

Thoughts on Landscape Painting

invite exploration and discovery of the areas around the focal point, eventually returning to it. This subtle guidance may be seen when you observe someone captivated for many moments by one painting, then glancing only briefly at another right beside it.   Goerschner

Horizontal movement relates to the parallel plane or level of the horizon and reaffirms the dominant horizontal directions of the painting surface. A bare canvas placed horizontally gives a sense of solidity because of its broad base. Horizontals also give an expansive feeling, and a painting composed through horizontal lines will make the shape of the canvas look even longer horizontally.   Handell

Abundant vertical movement in the composition may create an insecure feeling in the composition, which can give the feeling of being top-heavy or even of falling.   Handell

Diagonal Movement

Diagonal movement is usually a powerful movement in a composition—often the key directional element to movement in many compositions. It has the power to pull the attention of the viewer up, down, or across the painting. It can continuously direct the eye toward the center of interest.   If the diagonal movement goes from the lower left to the upper right, the eye will ride this diagonal movement upward, for we read from left to right and are used to viewing things that way In like manner, if the diagonal movement starts on the upper left and goes down to the lower right, the eye would be led downward.   Handell

Cezanne also played line against line. If he had a lot of round fruit in a picture, he'd have a lot of sharp, triangular shapes in the background draperies. Those harsh lines explained the round ones and made the fruit seem more like fruit.
Gruppe 1976

Thoughts on Landscape Painting

In geometry, there are right angles, obtuse angles, acute angles. In designing paintings, there are opposed and unopposed angles. There is an unopposed type of angle in which the lines of the angle are like railroad track in perspective. They simply meet at a point and the eye is like a train riding the lines of that track, going straight into the painting to the point of the angle where both rails meet. This is an unopposed, fast-moving angle. Opposed angles and combinations of opposed angles basically keep each other in check. There is generally more weight and more tension than speed to them. The opposed angles are worked into the design a bit like a tightly knit chess game, where things are balanced against one another.   Handell

Compositional tension refers to tightly knit paintings. It is unrelated to literal, or pictorial, tension, which receives its sense of tension from the subject and is illustrative. Compositional tension is a spatial sensation of "static" activity that creates a dynamically alive painting and can intensify the weight and communicativeness of a painting. This feeling can be created by the pull between planes, by their particular shapes, colors, tones, and textures, and by their placement in the painting.   Handell

Lines and shapes moving horizontally or vertically convey formality, solidity. Diagonals convey movement and excitement.   Brown

Visual Traps

"Visual traps" — lines, values, or shapes that meet at the same point (such as a tree, a road and the horizon)—can be detrimental to your composition. If your composition includes something with a strong perspective, such as a road, it's usually best not to show where the converging lines of perspective meet; otherwise, the viewer's eye is likely to follow the perspective path to a visual dead end at the vanishing point.   Reynolds

Thoughts on Landscape Painting

A line from edge to edge will pull the eye right through a painting. In fact, any line that touches the edge of the painting's format is a potential eye leak. A line touching the edge provides a ready exit for the eye right out of the picture by drawing attention to the edge.   Albert

In the suppression of corners the same instinct for the elliptical line should be followed because the composition, by avoiding the corners, will be described completely within its own space. Poore

A line that touches a corner of a painting is like a drain. Because the corner is where two edges (both places where the eye can drop out of the painting) meet, the outward pull is strong. Any line that directs the eye to a corner is an invitation to leave the picture entirely.   Albert

To keep the eye from following a line out of a picture, you need to use view blocks as well as eye magnets. A view block can be a line, shape or some other graphic element that stops the eye on its way toward the edge of the picture. It blocks the eye from following the path out of the picture and redirects it back in.   Albert

Providing two or more exits is a common error of bad composition. This is the main objection to balance on a central point, which produces two spaces of equal importance on either side. Poore

View blocks are usually placed close to the edge or in the corners of a picture. In a horizontal format, the blocks would normally be placed on the right or left edge, since the eye naturally follows the horizontal orientation to those edges. The eye is less likely to fall out the top or bottom. View blocks are more often placed in the lower corners than the upper ones.   Albert

Thoughts on Landscape Painting

The eye must contemplate the picture, returning from edge to center, but at no time should it be allowed to stick at the frame.   Carlson 1929

By using a combination of blocks and eye magnets you can keep the viewer's attention inside the picture.   Albert

The viewer's eye follows a definite path through the painting as it is scanned. Our job as artists is to make the path as interesting and as enduring as possible. We don't want to create an easy exit for the viewer's eye; we want to invite a long and pleasantly entertaining stay within the boundaries of the painting. We also want to create in the viewer the desire to return for another look. Albert

Don't do anything that attracts attention to the frame or border.   Don't crowd things into a corner.   Don't let shapes touch the edge of the frame.   Don't have faces or figures looking out of the frame.   Don't run lines into corners Albert

Corners are natural drains for the eye. Every corner of this painting has a diagonal leading the eye out of the composition.   Albert

Don't place figures seeing out. This naturally attracts attention outside the composition. Albert

Don't place shapes tangent to the edge   These tangents become unwanted focal points that lead the eye right out of the picture. Albert

Don't place lines leaning out   Don't direct the eye to the edge of the format with lines that thrust away from the center of the painting.   Albert

Thoughts on Landscape Painting

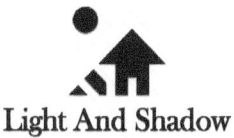

Light And Shadow

Light / Shadow Theory

Shadows which you see with difficulty, and whose boundaries you cannot define—but which you only apprehend and reproduce in your work with some hesitation of judgment—these you should not represent as finished or sharply defined, for the result would be that your work would seem wooden. Da Vinci 1452-1519 MacCurdy

Without light, there is no form. Light has several qualities that you must consider when lighting form — color, strength and location. Simply put, a warm light intensifies warm objects and neutralizes cool objects. A cool light intensifies cool objects and neutralizes warm objects. McCaw
Among shadows of equal strength that which is nearest to the eye will seem of less density. Da Vinci 1452-1519 MacCurdy

The exact relation of the colours of the shadows are to the colours of the lights, so that they may be at once felt to be merely different degrees of the same light. The want of tone in pictures is caused by objects looking bright in their own positive hue, and not by illumination, and by the consequent want of sensation of the raising of their hues by light. John Ruskin - Painters I 1857

Describing form is not a function of shadow. Leffel

Those trees and shrubs which are more split up into a quantity of thin branches ought to have less density of shadow. The trees and the shrubs which have larger leaves cast a greater shadow. Da Vinci 1452-1519 MacCurdy

Thoughts on Landscape Painting

A picture should be laid-in as if one were looking at the subject I on a grey day, with no sunlight or clear-cut shadows. Fundamentally, lights and shadows do not exist. Every object presents a colour-mass, having different reflections on all sides. Suppose a ray of sunshine should suddenly light up the objects in this open-air scene under grey light, you will then have what are called lights and shadows but they will be pure accidents. This strange as it may appear, is a profound truth and contains the whole meaning of colour in painting. How extraordinary that it should have been understood by so few of the great painters, even among those who are generally regarded as colourists.   Delacroix 1798-1863 Wellington

Light / Shadow Contrast

Establish your shadow pattern first, even though they will change rapidly outdoors. Painting the shadow shapes first is very important to assure clean bright color and a consistent pattern of light.   MacPherson

Light and dark values that are close to each other tend to express an airy or soft quality. Leffel

Light comes first and foremost.   Whisson

Shadow means the absence of light; it is an absolute. Yet shadows are rarely totally dark
because light is usually reflected into them from nearby objects. But reflected light does not always result in making shadows light. Sometimes it makes the shadow appear darker by contrast. Leffel

Placing Light and Shadows

Place shadow shapes before light shapes for more control, looking at the color of shadows carefully to see how they reflect the sky or nearby objects, and how they contrast in

Thoughts on Landscape Painting

both temperature and value with the light family. MacPherson

A cast shadow usually becomes lighter, and more soft-edged, the farther it is from the object that's casting the shadow. Brown

Mass in the shadows on all your objects first. Then apply local color as, for example, the orange and yellow on oranges. For the transition color between the shadow and the local color, you can pick up the color of the air background. Leffel

Parts of a painting may be subordinated by the use of cloud shadows -"the painter's friend." Strisik

It is easier to gain control over light family colors by first placing all the shadow shapes accurately. What are the shadow shapes? MacPherson

The anatomy of an Impressionist painting Light coming from behind the artist, and midday light, with its harsh, bleaching effects, are the preferred conditions.   Whisson

Observing Light and Shadow

Darker material has darker shadow, lighter material has a lighter shadow. Leffel

Cast shadows provide an object with roots and stability and keep it from floating in midair. They are an important structural unit. They help describe the surface the object rests on. Leffel

Since the sun is constantly moving, establish a single direction and color for the sunlight in your painting. Keep sun-side (light family) shapes separate from shade (shadow family) shapes. MacPherson

Thoughts on Landscape Painting

In the shadow areas and the background, try to keep the values close together. Leffel

Darks get lighter as they go further back. Light is more constant outdoors as well as indoors. Leffel

Think before you put in reflected light. It should be added for a pictorial purpose. Don't just put it in automatically. Leffel

Shadow Color

I advise you to put color in the shadows, because this is the secret to greater depth. The more depth you can get in the shadows the better.   Whisson

To understand shadows, don't worry about their different colors. Instead, think of all the shadows in your picture as related by the fact that they're devitalized forms of energy. They all share a hint of our most devitalized color, violet. Put down the darks with a poster-like simplicity, thinking more about value than color. Strisik

The anatomy of an Impressionist painting - Introducing color into the shadows is important.   Whisson

Remember that each shadow in a painting should have at least one hue in common. Even if the objects in your scene are different colors (and therefore have different-colored shadows), at least one color should recur in every one. Krieger

Make a richer statement with your shadows. Use more cadmium colors—yellow, orange, red—with ivory black. Cadmium colors create depth because they make things transparent and the eye equates depth with transparency. Opacity is the look of light. The more cadmium you use, the more space you create. In place of ivory black, you can use umbers or blues. Leffel

Thoughts on Landscape Painting

Place shadow shapes before light shapes for more control, looking at the color of shadows carefully to see how they reflect the sky or nearby objects, and how they contrast in both temperature and value with the light family.
MacPherson

If you have a lot of light, take out some of the color. Don't have both light and color competing for your attention. In other words, in a light area, paint color or light. Leffel

Values

Value Theory

Color is easy, value is difficult. Leffel

Anything in sunlight is lighter in value than everything in shadow regardless of the color, value or texture. Charles Reid - Workshop

Even though full scale in pigment is used, the relation of values within each mass in the picture must be very much closer than those outdoors. Payne 1941

Drawing alone can't fix a piece, the values have to be working. OPA David Dibble
Most good pictures are produced in the medium tonal range. A series of gradations in which a graceful flow of line and tone is blended with a forcible stroke will result in a combination of subtlety and strength. Poore
Now the finely-toned pictures of the old masters are, in this respect, some of the notes of nature played two or three octaves below her key; the dark objects in the middle distance having precisely the same relation to the light of the sky which they have in nature, but the light being necessarily infinitely lowered, and the mass of the shadow deepened in the same degree. I have often been struck, when looking at a camera-

Thoughts on Landscape Painting

obscura on a dark day, with the exact resemblance the image bore to one of the finest pictures of the old masters; all the foliage coming dark against the sky, and nothing being seen in its mass but here and there the isolated light of a silvery stem or an unusually illumined cluster of leafage.   John Ruskin - Painters I 1857

The great paintings are the ones with the most subtle value relationships. The closer you could bring your values and still distinguish between them, the stronger you were as a painter. Carlson 1929

In painting as in life, you can get away with a great deal as long as you have your values right.   Brown

With the painter, the local color has very few thrills. Almost anyone can see local color. It is in the bright light or in the deep shadows, and the transitions between these, that the painter finds interest. Here he has to use all his analytical senses, together with his sight, to find their component parts. Too vague a colorcast, too undetermined a value and the desired unity is threatened, perhaps even the form annihilated.   Carlson 1929

Most brighter colors come to full intensity in mid-value. Webb

The masters who maintained simple value patterns in their paintings seldom used more than five values (except in the transition zones and soft edges between shapes). You can see this dramatically in black and white reproductions of works by Howard Pyle, Serov, Vandyke, and others. They were stingy with the number of tones they used and never employed more than were necessary. In many of his portraits, Sargent usually employed only three values in the light, two in the darks, and then added some incidental highlights and dark accents.   This economy or conservation of values is based on two ideas. The first is that a few clear-cut values in a

Thoughts on Landscape Painting

painting will yield a more powerful visual effect (though not necessarily a more "artistic" one) than a profusion of small values. That is why Impressionistic painting, which as a rule pays little attention to strong value patterns, is not as effective in monochrome reproduction as it is in full color. The second idea is that it is unnecessary to use all values in a subject. Color changes can frequently be used instead. Schmid

Always try to conserve your values. That is, use as few different values as possible. You can put in subtle value differences later. The range of values is usually the first thing a student uses up. Make warm or cool color changes rather than value changes. Leffel

A painting must have a dominant value; either it's light, or it's medium, or it's dark. Brown

Choose a range of values that suits the mood you're after. Paintings that have a lot of contrast are typically very active and generate a feeling of excitement. Paintings possessing a smaller, more limited range of values, on the other hand, tend to be more mysterious and inviting. Mitchell

Another important consideration when developing a value distribution pattern is the size of the area that each separate group covers. For a good balance and feeling in a picture, make sure either the dark or light areas occupy more picture space. Smuskiewicz

Don't feel you're limited to reproducing the values exactly as they're found in your subject. Be reasonable in exaggerating or manipulating your values so that you retain a sense of realism, but also challenge yourself to find a more interesting solution that makes the most of how we see tonal values. Mitchell

Thoughts on Landscape Painting

I would first try to work out logically the different values, in their nearer or more distant relationships, according to spatial and aerial perspective. There can be no sharp definition, no linear structure in something that is all movement; only tonal values which, it correctly observed, will constitute its true volume, its essential, underlying design. Manet, 1987, Wilson-Bareau

Value Contrasts

The character of everything is best manifested by Contrast. Rest can only be enjoyed after labour; sound, to be heard clearly, must rise out of silence; light is exhibited by darkness, darkness by light; and so on in all things.   John Ruskin - Elements 1857

Tonal painters were reserved in their color and sparing in their contrast. If Carlson were working on a clear day, he'd never use a pure white for the sunlit snow. The snow would be light in value,   but always slightly grayed - so that the lights and darks together as a unit when you at the picture. You knew Carlson could go lighter in the lights darker in the darks. You sensed the reserve behind the work, and that made it wonderful to look at.   Christensen

Establish your lightest lights and darkest darks near the beginning. This will make it much easier to place the relative values between them.   Brown

Don't become snarled in too many small values and over-modeling. They are fussy and thwart breadth. Webb

Make an interesting tonal plan that includes very dark and very light tones.   Whisson

The value of a black or a white unit is proportionate also to the size of the space that contrasts with it. Poore

Thoughts on Landscape Painting

Omit unnecessary values. Look at the subject and/or the painting with a black mirror. It is made of a simple piece of glass or Plexiglas with a black backing. This crude mirror reflects a low-key version of the image with emphasized variations of light values. All values below halftone run together in blackness—instant Rembrandt! Webb

Lead the viewer to the focal area with extreme value contrast. Introducing a "foreign element" in the form of a contrasting value can effectively grab a viewer's attention and guide it to a particular area. Mitchell

Unless it's your intention, be wary of using too many middle values; otherwise, your value plan and painting will lack snap and drama. Reynolds

The lightest light and the darkest dark set the value range and key of your painting. The key of a painting is like the key of a piece of music; you can play a song in the key of C or the key of E, but it is still the same music, just higher or lower. Painting is similar; you can start your painting warmer, cooler, lighter or darker. It's up to you. When painting in a high key (light), you need to establish your darkest dark much lighter than it appears. In a low-key (dark) painting, the lightest light will be darker. Your value range will probably be narrower in a high- or low-key painting, but the same principles of relationships are applied. MacPherson

Beware of making the darks too dark in a light painting. Brown

Often, of course, in the search for a punchy, dramatic effect, it is a good idea to pitch the whole canvas in a low key (a little darker than the eye appears to record), in this way allowing a successful emphasis to be placed on any light notes and areas which may occur. The higher the key, the less the tonal contrast, and to maximize an effect in this case, an emphasis

Thoughts on Landscape Painting

on the careful matching of tonal blocks relative to and in
harmony with each other is a definite advantage.   Curtis

Values within one dark or middle-toned area, for instance,
can be brought even more closely together, so that they
become almost the same. One whole area of tone can be run
into another in this way, and parts of the picture can be
connected.   Dunstan

Dark has a lot of weight to it. Apply it thinly. Light is more
buoyant. Apply it more thickly.   Brown

Hit your darks hard. You may even want to exaggerate them.
The sooner you put down the darkest dark, the easier you'll
be able to decide how strong to make the rest of your lights
and darks. It gives you a standard. By keeping the dark low in
key, you'll get good contrast and won't have to exaggerate your
lights. Then, you'll have something in reserve when you put
your highlights in.   Gruppe 1976

The painter who is sensitive to tonal relationships and pattern
will compose his areas of tone so that they fall into groups,
each of which contains closely-related values. This may be a
matter of very small adjustments, deriving from very exact
observation.   Dunstan

Value Placement

Place a middle value first for a better grasp of the whole
gamut of value and to reveal lights. Then add darks. The
darkest value of shade is found just before it turns into light.
Webb

An equal distribution of light and dark values is static and
lacks emphasis. Use a variety of values to make your
underlying abstract designs definitively lighter or darker.
Reynolds   Isolated spots of light and dark values can create
unintentional emphasis, which, in turn, can lead to tension

Thoughts on Landscape Painting

and confusion. Group and connect major shapes and values. Large, bold shapes result in stronger designs than small, isolated, "busy" arrangements of shapes and values.   Reynolds

Don't put darkest or lightest values at the edge of the painting. They more properly belong at the center of interest. Don't go so anxiously for high-lights and the accents without using that great body of mid-value. Webb

Be sure to separate your big values with differentiated steps. "The unreadable will shortly be unread."–Jacques Barzum. Webb

Try to create visual paths that will repeatedly lead your viewer's eye around the painting instead of trapping it in some corner or pulling it right out of the composition. By paths, I mean shapes of light or dark values that visually "link up" vertically, horizontally or diagonally through a composition. Mitchell

Give most of your attention to the four to seven largest pieces of value in your painting. If these few large hunks are not the most distinguished shapes you can make, your picture will fail. Webb

Avoid making the values of adjacent shapes too similar; otherwise, they may mesh together and interfere with the illusion of depth. If an area, such as a group of foreground rocks, becomes too "busy," then reverse the process and use close values to subdue it and allow the forms to mesh. Reynolds

One way to avoid making too many value changes as you add details is by making color temperature changes instead. Leffel

As you lay in your big tonal areas, don't pay attention to the numerous shifts in value within a mass. The area will be filled

Thoughts on Landscape Painting

with halftones and quarter- tones, but you could spend all day trying to record them. Just put it down, either light or dark. The simpler the better.   Gruppe 1976

A device that should be mentioned here is that which is known technically as counterchange. This refers to the contrast created by two (or more) silhouetted forms, one of which is light against dark while the other is dark against light. Dunstan

Value Gradation

When value gradations are used to render light on a curved surface, get more spunk into the surface by making a series of harder-edged value steps (French blend). It is especially useful when working in gouache. Webb 1994

Space without detail may possess attraction by gradation and by suggestion. Poore

It is a good thing to get into the habit of working with a few tones (this example uses about four gradations of dark, plus a white, on a middle- toned paper). Allow similar tones to connect together, while emphasizing the contrast between different ones which meet, such as the man's bent back against the trees on the right.   Dunstan

Thoughts on Landscape Painting

Color

Color Theory

Josef Albers - Every color goes with every other color if the quantities are right.   Audette

Most brighter colors come to full intensity in mid-value.   Webb

"Good color" in a picture, means not at all that certain prettiness that the vulgar demand. It means expressive color with its infinite variations, not merely color "dashed in" upon the canvas! Good color really means good taste; and "powerful" color means a reserve, to give a climax its full force, and not "red, white, and blue all over." Carlson 1929

Design is the choosing and placing the colour so as to help and enhance all the other colours it is set beside.   John Ruskin – Paths 1857

Successful use of color in painting will come with study. Ultimately, a picture should be so well synthesized or organized in color that, were it turned upside-down (the subject matter thereby becoming unrecognizable), the color relations and transitions would in themselves (as abstract color) express the idea of the picture.   Carlson 1929

No one yet however, has been entirely successful in attaining a completely "natural" result. By this I mean that impressionistic broken color paintings are (by definition) departures from the way most humans see the world. If you or I actually saw things entirely as discrete patches of exaggerated color, it would indicate some form of visual impairment   Schmid

The anatomy of an Impressionist painting - Color is not premeditated.   Whisson

Thoughts on Landscape Painting

Warm colors advance and cool colors recede. The human eye expresses a natural preference for yellow, red, orange; it sees gray, blue, green only peripherally.   Leffel

It is a favorite dogma among modern writers on colour that ' warm colours ' (reds and yellows)' approach ' or express nearness, and ' cold colours ' (blue and grey) ' retire ' or express distance. So far is this from being the case, that no expression of distance in the world is so great as that of the gold and orange in twilight sky. Colours, as such, are absolutely inexpressive respecting distance. It is their quality (as depth, delicacy, etc.) which expresses distance, not their tint.   It is quite true that in certain objects, blue is a sign of distance ; but that is not because blue is a retiring colour, but because the mist in the air is blue, and therefore any warm colour which has not strength of light enough to pierce the mist is lost or subdued in its blue. John Ruskin - Elements 1857

But remember, never make any plane so white that it cannot be made whiter. Alberti 1436 Spencer

There is, however, I think, one law about distance, which has some claims to be considered a constant one: namely, that dullness and heaviness of colour are more or less indicative of nearness. All distant colour is pure colour: it may not be bright, but it is clear and lovely, not opaque nor soiled; for the air and light coming between us and any earthy or imperfect colour, purify or harmonize it; hence a bad colourist is peculiarly incapable of expressing distance.   John Ruskin - Elements 1857

With the painter, the local color has very few thrills. Almost anyone can see local color. It is in the bright light or in the deep shadows, and the transitions between these, that the painter finds interest. Here he has to use all his analytical senses, together with his sight, to find their component parts.

Thoughts on Landscape Painting

Too vague a colorcast, too undetermined a value and the desired unity is threatened, perhaps even the form annihilated.   Carlson 1929

Most successful paintings have a dominant color.   Brown

A line or a value may be absolutely wrong but color is always relative. Webb

Charles Hawthorne summed up the whole painting activity as "putting one spot of color next to another." Webb

Take time mixing the first color note you put down, because all of the others will have to relate to it. It's all relative, so get the first color as accurate as possible.   MacPherson

Synthesis in colour.—Colour requires higher power of synthesis than anything else in art, for although analysis is of use in studying natural colour, it does not of itself enable us to make colour of our own; because, whether you will or not, in painting on any one part of your picture you are really painting upon, that is, changing the colour of, the whole canvas at once, and unless you do this always synthetically you will never succeed. Every new touch changes all the touches already laid,—if warmer it cools them, if cooler it warms them, if brighter it dulls them, if duller it lends them brightness. This is so curiously true that visitors to the studios of painters constantly believe that the artist has been working on portions of his picture which he has never touched since their previous visits. And they are right. Hamerton 1882.

Color of Light

Yellow is the color of transmitted light. It will make almost anything look transparent, especially shadows. Orange and red also bring about these results, but yellow more so. When you're painting leaves, or paper, if you put enough yellow in the shadows, it will make them look transparent.   Leffel

Thoughts on Landscape Painting

This happens—ALWAYS whether it is the sun, the full moon, a table lamp, or even the dizzy neon lights of big cities—the source of light, or any combination of sources, produces a predominating effect that influences the color of everything in sight. The color of the light acts as a common denominator to visually unite everything it illuminates.   Schmid

The color of light falling on all the different colors will unify them. Leffel

Make a distinction in your mind between painting light and painting color. Each requires a separate brushstroke. You cannot paint light and color at the same time. The more light you have on a surface, the less color that surface will have. Leffel

Adding white to a color is the only way of making it lighter. So far so good, but what also happens is this—when we add white to any color or mixture, we also cool it. This happens because white is the "coldest" pigment on our palette. It lowers the "saturation" of any color it is mixed with. Fortunately, this works to our advantage when we work in cool light because colors on a subject get cooler as they get lighter—the same thing that happens when white pigment is added to colors. Cool light then works with our mixtures. This is one of the reasons why many artists prefer cool overcast north daylight. Here are a few more things to observe: Schmid

Don't worry too much if you don't have full-spectrum light or north light in your studio. Your work will hang in someone's normal room lighting. Of course, good lighting is desirable if possible. Under incandescent light, yellows and oranges are intensified while blues and purples are weakened. Out- doors in daylight, these effects are reversed. Webb

Thoughts on Landscape Painting

The anatomy of an Impressionist painting - Warm and cool color juxtapositions are used to evoke form instead of the tonal modeling method.   Whisson

A color's complement is the same as its afterimage. This is found by looking at a color for half a minute and then looking at a white background. Because complements produce gray, a near-complement offers a wider range of color effects. This arrangement may result in the same neutrality as a complementary scheme since the two near-complements together equal the complement. Webb

Selecting Colors

Pick the easiest color to put down; that is, the easiest color to get right without a lot of mixing.   MacPherson

If the colour is wrong, everything is wrong; just as, if you are singing, and sing false notes, it does not matter how true the words are. John Ruskin - Elements 1857
But in the far distance that object will show itself most blue which is darkest in colour.
Da Vinci 1452-1519 MacCurdy

A sallow colour makes another which is placed beside it appear the more lively, and melancholy and pallid colours make those near them very cheerful and almost of a certain flaming beauty." Vasari. 1568   Craig

Colour is wholly relative. Every hue throughout your work is altered by every touch that you add in other places; so that what was warm a minute ago, becomes cold when you have put a hotter colour in another place.   John Ruskin - Elements 1857

Discard black and that mixture of white and black they call grey. Nothing is black and nothing is grey. What seems grey is

Thoughts on Landscape Painting

a composite of pale tints which an experienced eye perceives.
*Gaug*uin (1848-1903)

Too much intense color can ruin a painting, because the colors will appear to fight each other for attention. Graying down or watering down a complement will allow you to use more of it.   Brown

A color needs its complement in order to exist. A red isn't a red without a contrasting green to explain it. Carlson 1929

You'll be surprised how little cool color is necessary to make the sky look natural. Students almost always use too much blue! They kill the sunlight effect. It's the warm color that counts; the less blue you use, the better.   Gruppe 1976

Every so often change your palette. Introduce new colours and discard others.   You will gain knowledge of colour mixing and your work will have added variety. Denton

White is the coolest color. Adding white to another color will make that color cooler. White also adds opacity. Leffel

Keep all the color notes in the light family lighter than the shadow shapes. Lay them down flatly and simply. Cover the whole canvas, thinking about shapes. Step back and recheck your color choices. Don't be in a hurry to produce a finished painting.   MacPherson

Using a limited palette has been a tremendous benefit to my art. Now that I'm familiar with how my six colors and their temperature relate to and affect one other, it's easy to allow the creative process of painting to take oven The built-in simplicity and consistency of my method makes me think less about the technical side of what I'm doing and permits my intuitive responses to come through and reveal more about me. Arsenault,

Thoughts on Landscape Painting

Limiting my palette to the same shades throughout an entire painting creates a color harmony that pulls the various compositional elements together: Akers

It is a very poor habit to pull all colors back with blue. Bluishness all through the canvas is a sign for atmosphere. The neutrals of any color scale will pull a tone down toward neutrality. Sloan (1871-1951)

What color is the lightest light? Never use pure white, but white with a small amount of color in it.   MacPherson

Now I'm well aware that not one of the flowers has been properly drawn, that they are only small dabs of colour, red, yellow, orange, green, blue, violet, but the impression of all those colours next to one another is there - in the painting as in nature. Van Gogh (1853-1890) De Leeuw, Ronald

Simplify your palette by using six or fewer colors. This approach lets you mix any color relationships you want, and gives your paintings color unity. MacPherson
I believe that a painting requires strong tonal difference. It should have bold use of color. The compositional elements should be placed accurately so that the elements in the painting are balanced and the painting has a sense of natural grace. Whisson

One way to avoid making too many value changes as you add details is by making color temperature changes instead. Leffel

Placing Color

Try to keep your most vital and saturated color or color harmonies somewhere near the center of your design. If your arrangement of subject matter does not permit this, try to keep your most interesting or moving forms or lines near the center. Carlson 1929

Thoughts on Landscape Painting

In a great picture, every line and colour is so arranged as to advantage the rest. None are inessential, however slight; and none are independent, however forcible. It is not enough that they truly represent natural objects; but they must fit into certain places, and gather into certain harmonious groups: John Ruskin – Elements 1857

Color beauty is arrived at only through sensitive juxtaposition of color masses, of varying proportions, of values and transitions. Carlson 1929

Whenever you lay on a mass of colour, be sure that however large it may be, or how- ever small, it shall be gradated. No colour exists in Nature under ordinary circumstances without gradation. If you do not see this, it is the fault of your inexperience. John Ruskin – Elements 1857
Try to keep your most vital and saturated color or color harmonies somewhere near the center of your design. (Not the dead center) If your arrangement of subject matter does not permit this, try to keep your most interesting or moving forms or lines near the center. Carlson 1929

The first piece of color and/or value you put down should make a definite statement. Otherwise, you will not be sure how the second statement relates. After the first piece of paint, or statement, is on the canvas, you can determine whether or not the second should be lighter or darker or have more or less color. Leffel

We must not train our eyes to copy tone for tone, but think of the bearing of such colors and harmonies upon the main idea of our picture! Carlson 1929

Place your color on the canvas and leave it alone. If you spread it and play with it, it will become muddy or chalky. Chalkiness is caused by having too much free-floating color in an area, not by using too much white as many students believe. The color has no boundaries and the eye of the

Thoughts on Landscape Painting

viewer is often unable to identify the area as even having a color. Leffel

The big test for any painter is how to place the big areas of color. I advise you to put color in the shadows, because this is the secret to greater depth. The more depth you can get in the shadows the better. Whisson

You can use a great range of color sequence to make signs for distance. A green in the foreground can be made to look like yellow-green when placed in the background among cooler and more neutral tones. You can paint a brown field all the way from semi-neutral yellow to semi-neutral red. Sloan (1871-1951)

The anatomy of an Impressionist painting - Impressionists put down the colors they saw, not the colors they knew. Large planes of color with little or no detail means there is nothing to detract from the broad composition. Whisson

The underpainting should be neutral and preferably cool in color. Positive colors may be underpainted with shaded tints of the full color. This is especially true of blues and reds because the oil glazes darken or fade. Reds are best underpainted with vermillion or cadmium. Greens with yellow, and so forth. The colored undertone supports and gives luminosity to the glazes. Sloan (1871-1951)

Don't put right color over wrong color. Better to first scrape or wash the wrong color away.   Since you probably have intervals of hue and value, now add intervals of intensity. Webb

There is no question about the power of grays to enhance the more pure colors. Schmid

Thoughts on Landscape Painting

Shift hue a little whenever a value changes. Hold the value
and change the color, and other times hold the color and
change the value. Webb

Any large area will likely improve with a gradation of hue,
value or intensity. Webb

When correcting the color of any mass, try to do it by laying
into it the correcting tones in small touches, and without
lifting the under paint up too much. Carlson 1929

Acres of clear color are muddied by touching areas too often.
Webb
Each time a brushload touches an area already wet with paint,
purity and brilliance are compromised. Once a color is set
down on a surface, it is difficult to add to its intensity except
when a thick layer is superimposed. Webb

Mixing Color

Therefore, the mixing of white does not change the genus of
colours but forms the species. Black contains a similar force
in its mixing to make almost infinite species of colour. In
shadows colours are altered. As the shadow deepens the
colours empty out, and as the light increases the colours
become more open and clear. For this reason the painter
ought to be persuaded that white and black are not true
colours but are alterations of other colours. The painter will
find nothing with which to represent the brightest lustre of
light but white and in the same manner only black to indicate
the shadows. I should like to add that one will never find
black and white unless they are mixed with one of these four
colours. Alberti 1436 Spencer

The anatomy of an Impressionist painting - Colors are under-
mixed, producing raw, vibrant effects. Whisson

Thoughts on Landscape Painting

Whatever the medium, try to avoid an over-mixing of colors both on the palette and on the surface. Webb

A lot of trouble with many painters today is that they paint either at one end of the palette or the other. Their pictures are either very cool - with lots of blues and greens or very warm - with lots of ochre and umber. They ignore the great modifier-RED. Gruppe 1976

Optical mixture adds mystery. Optical mixture takes place in the beholder's eye as it views the broken colors of pointillism, or layers of contrasting, transparent color. Webb
Color mingling is a good way to show the brilliance of color as well as the subtlety of color grays. In color mingling, colors are not totally mixed together. Some of the original hues remain separated, allowing a visual blending. Color pigments may be applied with a brush or painting knife, using wet-over-wet or wet- Smuskiewicz

Don't mix pure white in the sky to lighten it. That makes it look opaque. Use white with a little orange or yellow-orange, and so forth. Use whatever color change will help to make the horizon line a place where the form passes back rather than a painted edge. Sloan (1871-1951)

We do not normally see colors that way; we see them as already blended. We see green as green, not yellow and blue. (We must be trained to see it that way.) I do not suggest any criticism here of the Impressionists' efforts, but I do mean to point out certain limitations inherent in any "broken color" technique. Schmid

The more you mix, the less color you'll have. Resist the need to model everything in your subject. Think in terms of flat shapes, then concentrate on filling each flat shape with lively color. Afterward, work on adjusting the color within each so that all of the big shapes relate well.   McCaw

Thoughts on Landscape Painting

It is possible to enhance the appearance of paint mixtures by avoiding the habit of over-mixing. Colors that are mixed too thoroughly lack the brilliance of more loosely blended paint. Schmid

When mixing colors on your palette, don't mash the colors into each other. Try to paint the colors together with the same consideration you use to paint a delicate nuance on your canvas.   To change the value of black, change the temperature. Adding a warm color to black will make it look darker; adding a cool color will make it look lighter, at the same value. Leffel

You have all heard the saying about warm colors "advancing" and cool colors "receding" in landscape painting—that is simply false, so don't believe it. There are no such constants in nature. Sometimes colors appear cooler with distance, but not always. The idea that a color can be "neutralized" by mixing it with its complement isn't true either, because there is no such thing as a neutral color.   Schmid
However much you may use "broken color," hold on to the few simple larger masses of your composition, and value as most important the beauty and design of these larger masses, or forms, or movements. Do not let beauty in the subdivisions destroy the beauty or the power of the major divisions. Henri 1923

Color Harmony

The fewer colors you use, the more likely you are to have a natural harmony within the picture. Zorn - vermilion red, yellow ochre, black. Carlson 1929

The color of light falling on all the different colors will unify them. Leffel

A picture may embody almost any color scheme so far as "color harmony" is concerned. Objects drawn upon the canvas

Thoughts on Landscape Painting

may have almost any color for their local color. The question is, what color, or set of colors, best expresses our idea in a given picture. We must make a choice. Carlson 1929

The colors appearing throughout a subject often need to be harmonized. This can be achieved by allowing the color of the light to touch all of the elements or by mixing a common color/temperature into all of the elements.   McCaw
Limiting my palette to the same shades throughout an entire painting creates a color harmony that pulls the various compositional elements together: Akers

Get all your colors on the canvas quickly. Get them in front of your eyes so you can see how they relate. Determine your background color immediately, then the colors of the various element in your painting. You can then integrate everything for an overall look. Leffel

Perhaps the oldest, most time-honored, seemingly most plausible (and wrong) method of creating a harmonious color relationship is the practice of premixing a single color into every other color on the palette before starting a painting. Schmid

Previously mixing a large amount of dominant shade then injecting it in every color used is sometimes called the "soup" method, but whatever name it is given it is a great help not only in developing taste but in creating harmony. Payne 1941

To ensure your background colors will still look good when the painting is finished, it's best to paint the background at the same time you paint the subject. Waiting until the subject is complete to fill in the background often ruins the painting because we tend to judge colors based on how they look next to other colors. If you paint the subject first, you're likely to choose colors that look good alongside the color of the canvas

Thoughts on Landscape Painting

or paper as opposed to the colors of your background. Dawson,

Making surrounding areas grayer or neutral is still another way of enhancing a color and making it look stronger than it actually is. For greater unified color harmony, choose grays from the same hue or family as the color they surround. Smuskiewicz

Don't repeat a background color on the object. It would mean there is a hole in the subject and we see background coming through. The two areas would seem to be on the same plane. Webb

The balance between bright intense colors and grayer colors is also very important. Gray colors help to bring out the full impact of the stronger colors by acting as a support for them. They complement the intense colors with their neutrality. Smuskiewicz

Try putting a mother-color down over all or most of the support. Then paint frank color into it. Webb

Edges

Edge Theory

You and I focus our eyes in a uniquely selective way when we look at things in the course of our daily routines. Edges are the only visual tools I am aware of that can replicate that special way of focusing.   Schmid

The proper painting of edges—for it is in the meeting of edges that we are really concerned. Anyone can paint a fairly good value-mass or two, but their JUNCTURE is a thing requiring thought.   Carlson 1929

Keep your most interesting and/or sharp edges near or around your area of interest.   Christensen

Thoughts on Landscape Painting

A photograph harshly portrays the cut out edges of a tree against the sky, but when we stand amongst the trees, we see them move; we see them alive with motion and atmosphere. Even with no breeze you still see through them and the light consumes the edges vibrating with all the surrounding color. Christensen

THE CAUSES OF EDGES IN A SUBJECT
Here are the main reasons they appear the way they do:

A. The inherent shape of things.

B. The intrinsic ("local") value and color of things (like a yellow dress or black hat). Elements or shapes that are similar in value or color will appear to have a softer transition between them than elements which contrast, even though the real (physical) edge is the same.

C. The nature of things—what they are made of—clouds, curly blond hair, and the rear ends of ducks are likely to have softer edges than bricks or door frames.

D. The light—how strong, or weak, or diffused it is, and the angle it is hitting the subject. .

E. The atmosphere- how clear or murky it is.

F. Motion. To our eyes, things blur when they move.
Schmid

Change in edges: Use hard and soft edges. Soft edges give a duller look; hard edges are more vivid or brilliant. Leffel

In general, try to keep edges soft. Hard edges attract the eye. MacPherson

Thoughts on Landscape Painting

Variety of Edge. Edges around a shape need variety. There are only three kinds of edge: hard, soft, and rough. The best shapes use all three.   Webb

If triangles are unavoidable, soften the edges or stagger the form.   Reynolds

Avoid Parallel Edges. Foliage and cloud shapes should not parallel other elements in a picture. Nor should any topmost point or incident be positioned immediately above or below a bottommost point or incident. Avoid placing one shape or incident immediately across from another. The position of all shapes and incidents should shift and alternate.   Webb

Remember, edges are separations between different tonal and color areas of a painting. Sometimes they are well defined and at other times they seem to be lost and hard to find. Right now detail is not as important as establishing a solid foundation of tone and color   Smuskiewicz

Think of lines not as the edges of objects but as the boundaries of two value shapes.   Webb

The vast majority of edges in any subject will fall into the intermediate range between hardness and softness.   In our ordinary everyday seeing we are not usually conscious of hard edges in our peripheral vision, which is why they seem unreal when scattered throughout a painting. We are aware of hard edges at or near the point we focus on. Paint the hard edges located at the borders of your subject less conspicuously.   Schmid

A soft edge shows continuity. The softer the edge, the duller the look. A hard edge shows ending. The harder the edge, the more riveting your painting is in that area.   Leffel

One safe way is to hold your strongest edge in reserve until you are dead sure you need it.   Schmid

Thoughts on Landscape Painting

Edges on the lighted side do not start darker. When light hits a surface, it is as lit up at the edges as it is inside. Leffel

Creating Edges

How can paint be manipulated so that it duplicates the edges you see in your subject? Physically, there are really only three ways that I know of. Schmid

1. By degrees of blending (soft edges), or refraining from blending (hard).

2. By mixing and applying intermediate colors instead of blending.

3. Applying intermediate colors and blending them (carefully).

Loosen up some of the edges by painting across them, or scraping while the paint is still wet. By this means the shapes can begot moving- again. Now try to bring out what you consider to be important directions or rhythms by sharpening the accent on certain edges and forms. Dunstan

Regardless of your medium, don't get carried away with blended edges. Nothing weakens a work more than indiscriminate blending. Another safe tip—avoid painting thickly while you are manipulating edges. Schmid

Thoughts on Landscape Painting

www.ingramcontent.com/pod-product-compliance
Lightning Source LLC
Chambersburg PA
BHW031421210526
464CB00005B/1993